CINCINNATI
AND THE
BIG RED
MACHINE

TOP: The opening of Riverfront Stadium, June 30, 1970. *Left to right*, Commissioner Bowie Kuhn, Reds general manager Bob Howsam, National League president Warren Giles, Charles Feeney, Reds president Francis Dale, Mayor Eugene Ruehlmann. (Courtesy Eugene Ruehlmann) BOTTOM: Riverfront Stadium still noticeably incomplete, January 1970. (Courtesy Riverfront Stadium Management)

CINCINNATI

AND THE

BIG RED

MACHINE

Robert Harris Walker

INDIANA UNIVERSITY PRESS
Bloomington and Indianapolis

Manufactured in the United States of America

Library of Congress Cataloging-in-Publication Data

Walker, Robert Harris, 1924-

Cincinnati and the big red machine.
  Bibliography: p.
  Includes index.
  1. Cincinnati Reds (Baseball team)—History.
2. Cincinnati (Ohio)—History. I. Title.
GV875.C65W34   1988   796.357'64'0977178   88-45166
ISBN 0-253-32863-2
SIBN 0-253-21370-3 (pbk.)
      1 2 3 4 5   92 91 90 89 88

This book is for

MATT

himself a "pretty good jackhammer third baseman,"
who helped me appreciate the Red Machine;

for my Knot Hole teammates

THE HYDE PARK ERIES

and especially for their brides who,
together with a few other stalwart, beautiful, and
accomplished ladies,
see to it that the Queen City is what it is;

and for the old girl herself

CINCINNATI

Happy (200th) Birthday!

CONTENTS

List of Illustrations

PREFACE

This book is about America—only if you believe that baseball is the national game and the Midwest is the nation's true heart. Any objections?

During the 1970s, the Cincinnati Reds fielded a team that dominated the sport as had few other teams in any decade. Unlike other professional teams, however, they were presented with a deliberate effort to represent the predominant values of the city and its surrounding region.

That decade opened with the completion of Riverfront Stadium, an event that was a milestone in local sport but which also symbolized the culmination of years of planning for downtown renewal and waterfront reclamation. Cincinnati, a city with as prominent a history in planning as it boasts in baseball, reached twin summits during this decade. The extraordinary leadership on both sides of this cooperative enterprise—Robert L. Howsam, Eugene P. Ruehlmann—provides the decade with its own articulate historians.

As Johnny Bench says, Cincinnati is a city of jocks. Sport is a central part of the local culture, and baseball is at the city's sporting heart. The city uses and has used baseball in a variety of ways. The converse is also true. The high visibility of Cincinnati and the Reds in the seventies offers an ideal chance to:

reconsider the exploits of the Big Red Machine and examine what made them work, on the field and off;

listen to the men that created and managed this team and the men who kept it from falling apart;

ponder the way in which the city and the region are represented by the team;

use the playing field and the locker room to appreciate the attitudes and values of a certain part of the country.

The Midwest is different from the South, New England, and the East and West coasts. This is said often enough, yet it does little to hide the fact that America continues to be disproportionately represented by what goes on in New York, Washington, and Los Angeles. Futhermore, the Midwest is far from being one homogeneous stretch of heartland. The people who speak in these pages have no doubt that Cincinnati is not the Apple or L.A. They also tell you why it is not Pittsburgh, Cleveland, or Detroit. And why it may be most like St. Louis or Kansas City. In defining the Reds, there was also a need to define their particular region.

Those who don't know Cincinnati and its part of Mid-America are sometimes puzzled by the relative lack of confrontational headlines and public demonstrations. They assume from this that social change is dormant. Yet the comments here recorded give rise to some questions about equal opportunity and social justice. The quiet way, some think, does not necessarily mean the lesser way.

The answer to questions such as this—if there is an answer —does not lie within the confines of Riverfront Stadium. If there is an answer, however, it will surely include what goes on at Riverfront. Anthropologist Clifford Geertz, in his classic "Deep Play," has persuaded his readers that understanding Bali is impossible without first appreciating the national sport: cockfighting. Thousands of voices have spoken on the utility of the national game as a key to understanding America: voices as different as the urbane and illusive Marianne Moore and the pungent hill sounds of Dizzy Dean.

What has escaped us is that baseball, wherever it is played, is *not* necessarily the same game. One of the great services of Robert Whiting's *The Chrysanthemum and the Bat* is to show how differently the "American game" can be played in another culture. Thus, at a time when the Reds were offering a distinctive style, this style was in some few ways closer to that of the Yomiuri Giants than to the style of the Oakland Athletics.

We all recognize different types of baseball—the long ball versus speed and finesse, for example—but we don't associate them with any particular part of the country, and probably we shouldn't. But this is not to say that the game itself does not have a different relationship to each local community.

Cincinnati is proud of its football teams: the Bearcats, Musketeers, and Bengals. It is close to Indiana, where basketball has long been the king of sports. But there is no question that the Queen City puts baseball first: in its networks of amateur teams; in its role in making the city the focal point of a region; in the function of its new ballpark in revitalizing downtown. Cincinnati not only gives baseball primacy, as Mayor Ruehlmann and Dave Parker both observe, but it uses baseball in some special ways. The city and the game keep inventing one another.

The city also has a characteristic way of playing the game of politics, economic development, and social change. In the pages that follow are many hints as to the origins and distinctiveness of this style. It is associated primarily with the Midwest but also with a region that has complex and important connections with the South. It takes the work ethic to extremes. It relies on heavy, voluntary support of the community—broadly defined—but equates this more with self-interest than with charity.

A recurring theme is the German heritage. There is little intent to equate the city with Germany or any part thereof. What seems to be celebrated are the qualities associated with the nineteenth-century German emigrés who brought with them an exceptional devotion to work, craftsmanship, church, family, and community. One hundred fifty years in the Ohio Valley have left some of the attributes untouched; others have evolved into no-nonsense business ethics, high professional standards, respect for efficiency, and civic pride. Strong Jewish, Roman Catholic, and Protestant temples and churches are expected to serve as cornerstones of society. And through all this dedication and hard work have been lovingly preserved the beer and the music, the associations and the festivals.

There is in this region a very thin veneer of tolerance for the pretentious, the insincere, the nonconformist. There is a distinct preference for solving social and economic problems deliberately—often behind the scenes—without allowing them to become hard, public political isues. It is a place where the nastiest thing you can call someone is a "do-gooder," and the fondest greeting is "you old son-of-a-bitch."

This is a book of opinions, not of facts; of questions and points of view, not conclusions. In assembling this material, I have not presented myself as an expert on urban or local history, on planning or on baseball. As a social historian I have been intrigued by certain contradictions. Exploring the patterns of social change in America—as I have been doing for the past twenty years—I was always aware of some disjunction between what textbooks take to be national patterns and what, in fact, seems to be going on in Cincinnati and in other parts of the Midwest. This topic gave me the chance to look again at a part of America that was personally familiar but which I sometimes had trouble locating as a scholar.

My only real advantage in approaching this topic—and it is a huge one—stemmed from having spent the first eighteen years of my life in

Cincinnati. Not that I have ever learned that much about the city and its history, but I did inevitably experience a lot of the things I hear others depict. As for baseball, my father and my Uncle John took me to my first game when I was eight. The scorecard (of course I still have it!) tells me I could have bought a two-pants suit that summer for $17.50 and that Dazzy Vance and Van Lingle Mungo subdued Chic Hafey, Babe Herman, and Ernie Lombardi with enough success to win two. Before long I had joined Powel Crosley's Knot Hole Club and fought for a seat in the right-field pavilion on "blue card days." All summer, laboring under the moniker of "Hub" Walker, one of the Reds' more forgettable outfielders, I gave my negligible best to the neighborhood team.

The backyard of our small house on Edwards Road featured the horse-shoe court where neighbors gathered every fine summer evening. Behind the steady clang of metal and the clink of ice were the voices of announcers from Bob Newhall and Red Barber to Waite Hoyt and Joe Nuxhall. We all assumed that the city's pulse would rise or fall with the fortunes of Alex Kampouris and Estel Crabtree, Lee Grissom and Johnny Vander Meer.

I do not cite these experiences as though they were exceptional. Rather, I assumed that they were universally shared, and I have tried to pass them on to my own children, and with some —not total—success. It still comes to me as something of a shock when I am confronted by a compatriot who does not see life as—in many ways—an extension of baseball. It is possible that, without this early and telling exposure to the baseball virus, I would have been hard pressed to understand a lot of the statements that follow.

The task of reentering the local culture was eased by many old friends, most of whom shared six years of Walnut Hills High School as part of what Gene Ruehlmann calls "that remarkable class of '42," which included his wife. Three were particularly helpful: Warren Hinsch, Jack Koons, and Reuven Katz. "Tots" Hinsch can stand at Fountain Square at noon and greet every third person by name. Maybe every second. He helped set up interviews and explained the background of public events. He allowed himself to be taken—in his own exaggerated way—as representative of the shifting feelings of sports fans.

Jack Koons, whom I have finally forgiven for introducing me to Waite Hoyt as "the eeriest of the Hyde Park Eries," was the president of Burger Beer and Midland Advertising during the height and decline of the era when radio networks dominated. Jack shrunk my ignorance a bit and steered me to others, such as the knowledgeable John Murdough, who continued the process.

In my private vocabulary, modern baseball is divided into "the age of Koons" and "the age of Katz." Reuven, one of the first lawyers to evince a sustained interest in representing athletes, had sat next to me in Ms. Yeager's eighth-grade homeroom and, on many an afternoon, joined in the murder of Shakespeare. He more recently helped me understand baseball in the age of agentry, arranged key interviews, and shared his marvelous box seats behind first base. Reuven was the first Cincinnatian to whom I mentioned this project; he was kind enough to encourage it.

Zane Miller, the University of Cincinnati's eminent local historian, furnished criticism and contacts. The best thing he did was to send me to Kevin Grace, UC archivist, who proved a true gold mine of information and viewpoints. Jim Ferguson, Reds Vice-President for Publicity, arranged the needed interviews and treated me as something less than the nuisance I surely was. I also appreciated the kindness of his colleagues Gordy Coleman, Connie Barthelmas, and John Braude.

Peg and Dave Ecker arranged an interview with Lou and Louise Nippert in their sumptuous owners' box one baseball evening and helped in many other ways. Jean Hawley went birddogging after information I needed. Ernest Eynon gave me a knowledgeable grand tour of the wonderful Gregory Thorp photos that adorn the Strauss & Troy corridors. Gregory Rhodes, of the Cincinnati Historical Society, helped with both words and pictures. Ray Zwick made possible the intelligent use of the *Cincinnati Enquirer*'s photo library.

In Kyoto, Phil Williams put Robert Whiting's stimulating book in my hands. Dennis Cashman, an observant visitor from England, urged the concept of America's Germanic nature. In Washington, my colleague Howard Gillette helped me through the urban and planning materials, while Bernard Mergen turned me on to Clifford Geertz and other works on sport and society. At the Library of Congress, Assistant Librarian John Broderick introduced me to the omniscient David Kelly, who gave me a thorough and intelligent bibliographical head start.

Without the flying fingers of "Fast Arne" Axelsson, I would never have escaped Uppsala with two chapters intact; and without the chance to chat with the resourceful Barry Jagoda, I would never have acquired an efficient title.

In Colorado, the Howsams permitted a visit while Bob was still recovering from a second hip implant. Not very mobile, Bob had to "hold still" for a long series of questions followed by a gracious dinner in the glass-roofed sunroom, where the season's first snow rustled above the commentary on the opening game of the League Championship Series. It was a warmly appreciated gesture.

For reading the text and making constructive suggestions, I thank Dan Rappaport and my old friend and one-time baseball announcer Astere Claeyssens. Tom Boswell, who followed the Reds as an exemplary sportswriter, gave me some distinctive and productive hints.

Having never interviewed anyone before, and scarcely knowing how to operate a tape recorder, I was predictably poor at the job. Most conversations I ended with, "Now what *should* I have asked you?" In spite of this lack of polish, I was treated with great patience, friendliness, and courtesy by virtually all the people I talked to: ballplayers, civic leaders, members of the media. The pages that follow make clear how much I owe to these individuals who, in truth, wrote this book. The importance of what Bob Howsam and Gene Ruehlmann had to say is obvious. Not quite so obvious, perhaps, is what I learned from Sparky Anderson, Johnny Bench, Ed Kennedy, and Brooks Robinson—nor is it obvious how much I enjoyed their congenial manner of dispensing wisdom.

Although one should never assume that physical power precludes mental prowess, we often do. Thus I might have been a bit taken aback when Big Klu turned out to be not just bright and observant but analytical and thoughtful beyond any comparable sources. I mentioned something along these lines to Sparky, who replied: "Oh, yes, he's the smartest guy I ever knew. You know those big *Times* crossword puzzles? He did them in ink!" It was with particular melancholy that I read first of Ted's retirement, then of his untimely death on March 29, 1988.

I owe the most to those who put up with the most: many thanks to Jack and Pat, Jean and Don, Bud and Carolyn.

CINCINNATI
AND THE
BIG RED
MACHINE

Prologue.....

ROSE ROUNDING THIRD

Rose is rounding third. It is a familiar National League scene as the spectators reflexively rise in their seats drawn helplessly toward the developing play at the plate. Rose's compact body gathers momentum, the arms pumping, the muscular legs churning, his feet skidding slightly as he makes the turn. The head begins to lower as this human projectile, driven more by will than by the skills of the sprinter, creates a blur of consummate action.

This particular dash, recorded on video tape, will be run and rerun as often as any moment in the archives of the sport. It will be remembered—with only slight inaccuracy—as punctuating the first game played in the Cincinnati Riverfront Stadium. It will be correctly recalled as providing an ending of unmatchable intensity for one of the most competitive of all battles between the stars of the two major leagues.

Although the first game had been played there two weeks before, the 51,838 spectators who attended the All Star Game of July 14, 1970, found a ballpark so new that it was in many ways unfinished. As the early innings of the game passed uneventfully, the media commentators offered—in words and pictures—the ancillary drama of a construction deadline and the rush to meet it. The scoreboard and sound system were still only temporarily in place; the plumbing was unfinished. The incoming fans had to be lifted onto the pedestrian bridges with portable escalators.

For a while this story was more suspenseful than the game as Palmer, McDowell, Seaver, and Merritt delivered five innings of goose eggs. Starting in the top of the sixth, however, the American Leaguers began to pick on Gaylord Perry and his successor, Bob Gibson, until they had piled up a 4–1 lead and even the loyal National League crowd was beginning to wonder whether a quick departure might not be better than a test of the postgame traffic patterns.

A crack of the bat froze them. Dick Dietz, a late-inning replacement for local favorite Johnny Bench, had blasted a Catfish Hunter slider over the 404-foot mark in center field. Singles by Harrelson, Morgan, and McCovey, surrounding pitching changes, gave Roberto Clemente the chance to tie the game, which he promptly did with a sacrifice fly off Mel Stottlemyre. Extra innings.

To this point the National League had won every overtime All Star Game; but their chances on this riverbottom July night looked no better than those of a catfish on the hook. Their hitters were having no success against Stottlemyre and Clyde Wright, while Claude Osteen seemed barely able to quell successive American League threats. When the first two NL batters again went out in the twelfth, it looked inevitable that the AL would soon break the deadlock.

Heads lifted, however, when Pete Rose stepped to the plate, assumed his deep crouch, and peered challengingly over his biceps at pitcher Wright. A native of Cincinnati, Pete had earned the moniker "Charlie Hustle" as he used his unique energy and absorption to blaze a fast trail through the farm system, joining the Reds in 1963 at the age of twenty-two. The last two years he had led the league in hitting, averaging over 200 hits and 100 runs. Connecting with a Wright delivery, Pete sprinted to first, where, as the ball landed safely in center, he made his sweeping turn and held up. The resulting roar incited a universal tingle at the top of the partisan spines while the American Leaguers reassured each other: "Two out. Just get one."

The Dodgers' Bill Grabarkewitz promptly lined to left, another two-out single, and up stepped the Cubs' Jim Hickman, halfway through a .315 season. NL expectations and the Riverfront decibels ascended in tandem.

Little thought was given to replacing Wright, a 6'1" lefthander. The seventh American League pitcher of the night, he was also one of the league's hottest, well on his way toward a fabulous 22–12 season for the Angels, allowing fewer than three runs per game. Hickman, 6'3" and right-handed, possessed a "book advantage"; but Wright had been having no difficulty retiring batters from either side of the plate in the summer of 1970.

With two outs and the potential lead run on second, the outfield pulled in, including Amos Otis, the capable Kansas City centerfielder whose throw following Clemente's fly in the ninth had just missed ending the game. Rose edged off second base, not pushing his luck. In spite of his hustle, Pete was not a speed merchant and had averaged fewer than ten steals a year in spite of a phenomenal number of opportunities. Never-

Pete Rose bowls over catcher Ray Fosse to score the winning run of the 1970 All Star Game. (Courtesy Archives and Rare Books Department, University of Cincinnati Libraries)

theless, as Hickman dug in against Wright, he edged onto the carpet and planted his left foot in the launch position; and, as Hickman stroked one safely over second, Rose was off.

Rose rounding third: a picture of energy and determination: the will to win incarnate. Every tendon in Rose's straining body told the watching world that he would score that run and get this bleeping game settled. It was a representation of the spirit admired by his townsmen to the point of eventually changing the name of the street outside the ballpark to Pete Rose Way.

Rose was rounding third and heading not just for home but for a human obstacle named Ray Fosse, Cleveland's 6'2" catcher, weighing 215 pounds and wearing the catcher's armor. Baseball's rules say that it is illegal to block the baseline without the ball; yet catchers are expected to wedge themselves into the area just up the third-base line from home, and hope that the throw will reach them before the runner's spikes clatter into the shinguard. Blocking the plate gives the throw the extra instant that often makes a decisive difference.

Glimpsing the dug-in catcher out of the corner of his eye, the runner showed no hesitation. Two out. This is it. Calling on the genes of his dauntless father—a man who played sandlot football into his fifties and once finished a game on a broken leg—Pete modified his trademark head-first slide into a downfield football block. Otis's accurate throw reached Fosse just as the head and shoulder of Rose slammed into the entrenched catcher, sending the two of them dazed and sprawling. However ungainly the resulting tableau, one thing was patently clear. The runner had touched the plate. Safe at home.

The game was over: 5–4 National League. Most of the fans left the park cheered by the fact that the stars of their league had again won in Cincinnati and again won in extra innings. Many on both sides were wondering out loud how a player could risk a headfirst, full-force assault in what is essentially a meaningless exhibition game. Those who knew Rose knew what his response would be: "Hey, is there another way to play this game?"

For this city the big event was showing off the new ballpark, a triumph coming only at the end of extensive controversy as to financing, location, ownership, and even its name. Emphatically downtown, the stadium made a clear statement about the city's determination to revive the central business district and to bring back to the "Queen City of the West" some of the eminence it had enjoyed in the days when river traffic made it a dynamic center.

The stadium itself was a climactic play in the contest for urban renewal. On this, its first large-scale exposure, the television cameras showed a full house, plenty of beer, sausage, and enthusiasm. And for a finale, the bonecrushing crash of the archetypical hardworking, determined home-town "Dutchman." Around the city's seven hills they had a hard time imagining a more fitting baptism for their new ballpark.

Chapter One.....
BACKDROP

The words that form the center of this book were spoken in the 1980s by people who know something about Cincinnati and its baseball team. They speak mainly about the 1970s. Yet their attitudes did not arise overnight. They acquire full resonance only when they are allowed to reverberate against the backdrop of the past.

Riverfront Stadium and the Big Red Machine grew out of an intimate relationship between the city and the sport. They were created within a region that is essentially Midwestern yet heavily conditioned, in matters of race as well as in matters of economics, by its position on the border of the South. These questions are as important in sport today as they were to the nation when the Red Stockings first pulled on their crimson hose. Cincinnati's priorities in the 1960s and 1970s reflect a long-nurtured need to balance progress with tradition, technology with human scale, professionalism with loyalty. The way the city views its heritage today has much to do with the way that heritage was perceived and nurtured a century ago. The city and the sport embrace one another today because of a long and intimate relationship during which the athletes were often taken as emblems of the city.

Town ball and baseball came to Cincinnati when it was in its early prime: prosperous and more famous than any other inland city. The city's latest ballpark came as a part of a "downtown renaissance," an era that students of the city have called an awakening. To appreciate the game, the city, and the relationship between the two, it is useful to look at a few events and to examine a few historic attitudes.

According to Harry Ellard, whose father left him the largest collection of records of the local game prior to the formation of the National League, town ball came to Cincinnati in 1860. The game quickly grew in popularity with the support of "our best men," including William Howard Taft, Nicholas Longworth, Aaron B. Champion, and Sir Alfred T. Goshorn (knighted by Queen Victoria for his kindness to British subjects while discharging his responsibilities at the Philadelphia Centennial Exposition of 1876). Local historians would find many familiar names in the Ellard scores, names such as Wulsin and Hickenlooper and Bellamy Storer.

The presence of leading citizens at the early games should not suggest any lack of overt enthusiasm. Ellard describes one close game featuring the waving of kerchiefs and parasols by the loyal ladies. At a crucial moment, one parasol came down on the head of a male partisan. The blow was sufficient to bring tears of pain to the man's eyes as the woman made her apologies. " 'Do not mention it,' he replied with gallantry, 'I suffer for a good cause' " (Ellard, esp. pp. 39, 87).

There is evidence that enthusiasm for the new game was not confined to the Queen City and its environs. Towns and villages strung up and down the Miami River made baseball their first sporting choice and invested inordinate pride in the outcome of the weekend games against the neighboring towns.

When local bragging rights are at stake, shenanigans can be expected, and imported "ringers" were not unheard of. One such, a traveling tooth-extractor, was master of a devilish spitball (what else from a dentist?), and he played in Ohio town games under more than one assumed name. This impostor was discovered, fined for his slippery pitch, and thrown out of the game; but not before he had accumulated enough material for a novel, *The Shortstop*. His real name was Zane Grey (Becker, in Spivey, pp. 77–93).

Zane Grey's case notwithstanding, Ellard claims that, in the amateur days, "it would have killed baseball to have brought in players from other cities." The club was a "local institution." The "best young men" took pride in playing on the team, and "men high in the business world" were proud to take care of the team's finances (p. 123).

Thinking still of the late 1860s and early 1870s, Ellard was uncompromising in his belief that the reputations of team and town were inseparable. In support of this belief, he quoted at length from a Cleveland newspaper, whose account of a Cincinnati visit makes up in florid eloquence what it may lack in hard news of the game:

> Since it has come to be that a State or city is in so important a sense represented by its leading baseball clubs, it must have been a gratifying thing to the visitors at the baseball grounds on Saturday to find that our State is represented abroad by a club so eminent in all amenities of good behavior and gentlemanly deportment, as well as sharp, unerring play. A body of lithe, well-formed young men, with clear, intelligent, manly faces, quiet and reserved on the field, and of unexceptionable morals, such

is the Cincinnati Club, the darling and pride of the city whose name it bears. Five hundred members, including many prominent gentlemen of the city, constitute its organization. Its games are watched and read over as the sensation of the hour, and the sturdiest voices as well as the daintiest of mouchoirs of Porkopolis are raised to celebrate its victories. (P. 112)

The arrival of baseball coincided with the rising sectional tensions that were leading precipitously to war. These tensions were painfully evident in the Queen City. Although most residents considered themselves unequivocal friends of Union, they also knew that their commercial livelihood depended directly on the South. The compiler of *The Cincinnati Almanac, 1840* argued emphatically for turnpikes and improved waterways connecting the city with the heart of Kentucky, where lay "large masses of coal, iron ore . . . also hogs, cattle, and an almost inexhaustible supply of wood for fuel" (Vexler, pp. 87–88).

Traffic with the South also meant involvement with slavery, a subject of extreme volatility. On July 23, 1836, "a very large and respectable meeting of the citizens of Cincinnati" convened at Lower Market House and passed with one voice a number of resolutions directed at the Ohio Anti-Slavery Society. Whereas the citizens recognized "the constitutional right of liberty of speech and of the press," they valued even more the "peace and tranquillity of our city." The elected president of the assembly, William Burke, appointed a committee of twelve, including former mayor Jacob Burnet and the ubiquitous Nicholas Longworth, to wait upon the leaders of the society and demand that the publication of their antislavery paper be discontinued.

Cincinnati is known to have served as a station on the "underground railway" that protected escaping slaves. It is also known as the site of the famous "Lane debates," which brought into the open the split of church leaders on the slavery question. It is not as well remembered that emancipation orators were not always well received in the city's public places, that the abolitionist "Lane rebels" lost their debate and moved north to Oberlin.

This confrontation in 1836 does not necessarily indicate a proslavery sentiment on the part of the city's leaders, or a disrespect for the First Amendment. Somewhere in the assessment of motives is the realization that Cincinnati was a border city doing business on both sides of the Mason-Dixon line.

The most obvious meaning of this meeting is doubtless the most important. Major decisions should not be made in that emotional climate the abolitionists were purposely creating. When James G. Birney, predictably, refused to suspend publication of the Society's *Philanthropist*, the citizens' committee reported that they had done their best and adjourned with a final wringing of hands in "their utmost abhorrence of everything like violence."

This sentiment survives. When, during the mourning of Dr. Martin Luther King, Jr., looting and pillage suddenly and almost accidentally erupted from a peaceful gathering, the police and fire departments quelled the disorder before it had wrought anything like the devastation visited on other major cities during this season of unrest. Within a week after this April 8, 1968, outburst, the city council had passed an "antiriot" ordinance giving the mayor or the city manager power to act without prior consultation with the council. In any future disturbance these officials would be expected to inform the sheriff and the governor, then call out appropriate force from any source to restore order with minimum delay.

The ordinance was not passed unanimously, but in most other respects it was reminiscent of the citizen reaction to James G. Birney's *Philanthropist* in 1836. The six Republicans who closed ranks to approve the 1968 ordinance were not necessarily belittling the importance of Dr. King or declaring civil rights a closed subject. They were providing a clear echo of their forbears' words 132 years earlier. In this community, incitement to disturbance is a crime; political and social issues will not be settled in the streets (Vexler, pp. 133–38).

Following the Civil War—and the incidental spread of baseball—the nation set itself in a businesslike attitude. Eventually "gentlemanly deportment" lost out to "unerring play." According to one historian of early baseball it was a group of businessmen "stung by embarrassing losses and anxious to foster civic pride" who founded baseball's first openly professional team. In other cities at least some players were being paid for playing and imported from outside. It is quite possible that some other city, had it not made a secret of its payroll, might have claimed the credit now unanimously bestowed upon the 1869 Red Stockings as the first professionals. It may be as revealing a clue to the nature of this city that, when it determined to end the "embarrassing defeats," it hired a complete team, a good team, and did so openly (Selzer, p. 7).

Pride in local talent, which had meant so much to Harry Ellard and the partisans of amateur baseball, was promptly sacrificed to aptitude. Of the first professional nine, only one (first baseman Charlie Gould) was a native son. The Wright brothers, Harry the manager and George the

TOP: Town ball and early baseball were amateur games for gentlemen. (Courtesy Cincinnati Historical Society) BOTTOM: The Red Stockings of 1869, the nation's first professional baseball team. (Courtesy Archives and Rare Books Department, University of Cincinnati Libraries)

shortstop, were from New York. The others were from New Jersey and southern New England. Harry, a part-time jeweler, put together a team that functioned like a well-made watch. They toured the nation from the Atlantic to the Pacific, attracting "well over 100,000 spectators," a remarkable feat considering the general absence of grandstands. Scores were unusually lopsided, the Red Stockings scoring enough runs in one inning to last a modern team for a week. Opponents often conceded after only a few innings trailing by twenty or thirty runs.

The climactic moment for this team came with its return to the true cradle of baseball, Greater New York, the original home of most Red Stockings. Here they faced the vaunted Mutuals, until then the undisputed rulers of the sport. The game, then hailed as the best ever played, came down to the final inning with the visiting team trailing. Two Red Stocking runs in the last of the ninth (in those days the first bat was determined by a flip of a coin) settled the issue. The resulting tumult in the Queen City found over two thousand celebrants milling around the Gibson Hotel "firing salutes, burning red flares, and cheering themselves hoarse." The players, on their return, were lionized; the club president said, no doubt truthfully, that he would rather head that ballclub than the entire nation (Allen, p. 5).

The Red Stockings went on winning. They were undefeated not only for all of 1869 but for half the next season as well, and lost their first game in circumstances that were dubious at best. That single defeat took away only some of their magic, and they continued to fascinate not only Cincinnati but much of the nation. Ellard credits this team with leading directly to the appointment of the first baseball writer, the first reporter to travel with a ballclub, and the first policy of publishing the results of games on a daily basis. Lee Allen says that the celebrity of the Red Stockings was "responsible, in many ways, for the founding, seven years later, of the National League" (p. 5). Clearly, baseball and Cincinnati put each other on the map.

No one claims that Cincinnati was the first city to merchandise its team, but there was, surrounding the legendary Red Stockings, an army of banners, medals, souvenir calendars, and song covers. The "ladies of the city" presented the team, at a public ceremony, with a white silk banner on which were embroidered scarlet stockings. The ladies thanked the team for making this emblem stand for "gentlemanly qualities," to which Harry Wright responded that, though the banner might not always float over a victory in the sport, it would always represent victory "over all temptations" (Ellard, p. 203).

A verse dedicated to the team declared:

We wore no mattress on our hands,
No cage upon our face,
But stood right up and caught the ball
With courage and with grace. (Pp. 172–73)

In the "year of the Red Stockings," 1869, Cincinnati began another enterprise equally distinctive and equally indicative of the city's character. It got through the state legislature a bill authorizing the city to construct a railroad line all the way from the north bank of the Ohio River to the city of Chattanooga, Tennessee. The city thereupon raised an $18 million bond issue, got permission from Kentucky and Tennessee, and, within two years, had begun construction of a 335-mile rail line that was to be a masterpiece of both engineering and urban development.

This singular "municipal railroad" was an answer to an obvious problem. The advantages bestowed on the city by the commercial prominence of the Ohio River were not being duplicated by the builders of railways. Cincinnati knew that its natural marketing area lay to the south. It had already become clear that no private entrepreneur was going to gamble on building a right-of-way over the formidable topography standing between the Queen City and its hinterland. Bridging the Ohio and raising the grade to match the nearby hills of suburban Kentucky was itself a major problem. Cutting through the Clinch and Cumberland ranges required so many tunnels that this part of the route became known as the Rat Hole Division. The bridge over the Kentucky River was another major achievement, winning for engineers J. H. Linville and L. F. G. Bouscared an international reputation.

In spite of monumental challenges, the line was completed for very close to the appropriated sum and was immediately leased to private operators, who named it, rather ambitiously, the Cincinnati, New Orleans and Texas Pacific Railway. The annual rent was $800,000 and was scheduled to rise by $100,000 every five years. Control of the line was placed in the hands of a board responsible to the city, and not to the railroad.

Under the terms of the lease, the investment was quickly amortized: in fact, it has continued to yield a tidy income used, among other purposes, for the development of the city's highways. Most important, it made that missing connection with the southern marketplaces. Soon the line was living up to its pretentious name and bringing in the intended business. This daring, imaginative, and singular venture did not return the Queen City to its phenomenal antebellum growth rate; but it kept the city from rotting on a defective transportation vine and made possible its continuing, diversified prosperity (Condit, pp. 61–66).

Late-nineteenth-century view of Cincinnati, with topography friendly to riverboats, unfriendly to railroads. Railroad bridge, *far right*. (Courtesy Cincinnati Historical Society)

Cincinnati was "hog butcher to the world" long before Carl Sandburg used that phrase in his poem about Chicago. In fact, in the nineteenth century, Cincinnati was doubtless called Porkopolis more often than it was called the Queen City of the West. Thus it was inevitable that when Josiah L. Keck, a prominent meatpacker, acquired the team, it would be called, to the dismay of many, the Porkopolitans. History does not record whether businessman Keck encouraged the nickname. Keck was fortunate enough to own the club in 1876, a year filled not only with Centennial celebrations of the nation's birth, but also with the historic founding of the National League. In spite of the intimations of stability and profit attendant on that event, the Reds did not do well during the Centennial year. The ballpark was not easily accessible, weather seemed inclement at the wrong moments, attendance fell.

As the man who hired a Jewish manager for a team called the Porkopolitans, Keck deserves some spot in history. When he took over the club, Charlie Gould, the only native on the famous Red Stockings, was in charge. In 1877 Keck replaced Gould with Lipman E. Pike, who is alleged to have been the first Jewish professional ballplayer. Neither Gould nor Pike was responsible for the rainouts or for the ballpark's inaccessibility, and neither was able to provide a remedy. So Mr. Keck's next move was passive. He lost interest in his plaything, dropped the ball, and left it where it lay, heading back to the slaughterhouse. This sequence of events led to a familiar Cincinnati response.

At the point of Keck's departure, the season was lost in every sense. There was no way the team could produce a winning record, much less capture the flag; and there was no way, short of gross manipulation, that the Reds' ledgers could be written in the black.

But residents of this city not only enjoy their baseball but feel that the city is judged by its baseball. The idea of the city's team failing to meet its commitments was therefore unacceptable. A group of eight "prominent citizens" promptly took over the management, paid Keck's debts, and saw to it that the team played out its schedule, at home and on the road: bloody, bowed, but not in default (Allen, p. 14).

Historians point to the "continental Sabbath" as an issue that caused social and political discord throughout much of the nineteenth century. The conflict arose from the pietistic insistence that Sunday be set aside as a day of tranquillity featuring worship and meditation. Opposing this view were the European immigrants who saw Sunday as their only day for song and revelry, whether at home or in public places. In Cincinnati, because of its settled population and German customs, the issue persisted well into the present century, involving the regime of Boss Cox in more than one squabble. In 1882 there occurred a series of events which show the prominence of this issue along with the city's peculiar combination of stubbornness and adaptability.

The Red Stockings had surrendered to prevailing fashions by avoiding Sunday games; but they could not afford to let the ballground miss its day of maximum revenue. So they rented it. Naturally, the tenants sold beer on the premises. Somehow this practice provoked a Worcester, Massachusetts, newspaper into a journalistic campaign against baseball and beer on Sundays, to which a local paper responded:

> Puritanical Worcester is not liberal Cincinnati by a jugful, and what is sauce for Worcester is wind for the Queen City. Beer and Sunday amusements have become a popular necessity in Cincinnati. (Allen, p. 21)

The city named for a sauce continued its campaign until the league was forced to act, which it did, expelling the Red Stockings from the National League. Cincinnati promptly helped organize the American Association, where it played a full and profitable schedule while the National League was having an off year. Not only did they make money, but they won the flag, playing two postseason, unauthorized exhibition games against the National League champions, Cap Anson's Chicago White Stockings. Each team won one game in what some consider to have been the first World Series, however unofficial and inconclusive (Allen, p. 21).

In 1887, Aaron Stern, president of the Reds, hired as manager a fiery, red-bearded man from Columbus. "It is doubtful," wrote Lee Allen, "if anyone could think of a name that would please the German residents of Cincinnati more than Gustavus Heinrich Schmelz." Schmelz lasted three years and turned in winning records. He might have brought home the flag if, ironically, he had not continuously met defeat at the hands of the St. Louis Browns and another "Dutchman," Chris von der Ahe (Allen, p. 33).

The 1890s were an important decade for baseball, and a number of key events had a Cincinnati setting. In the city during this period were Frank C. Bancroft, running the Reds' front office, Charles Comiskey, first baseman and manager, and Byron "Ban" Johnson, a sportswriter for the *Commercial Gazette*. Bancroft was a promoter par excellence and is credited with developing the Opening Day rituals which have, from his day forward, packed the ballpark regardless of the prior year's record. Opening Day soon became a special Cincinnati holiday, calling for expressions of civic pride through pageantry, and helping to perpetuate the distinctiveness of the first professional team and its city.

Comiskey was responsible for many innovations, including the positioning of the first baseman off the bag, the marking of coaching boxes, and the increase in umpires from one to two. Johnson, whose subsequent importance in organized baseball is voluminous, joined with Comiskey to found the Western League. This eventually became the American League, whose appearance paved the way for what is recognized as modern baseball (Allen, p. 45–52).

From the 1860s to the 1980s, the presence on Cincinnati baseball teams of native sons has been a matter of recurring interest. In this regard, one of the greatest "reunions" occurred in 1895, when William "Buck" Ewing was brought home at last. A native son, he had played eighteen years in the big leagues with a .311 average. Possessed of a fabulous arm, he could throw effectively from unorthodox positions and, in fact, became the first catcher to crouch behind the plate, bringing himself closer to the action. Connie Mack, a catcher himself, called Ewing the best he had ever seen.

Although he had played in the National League, it had been during that brief period when the Red Stockings had been exiled; so the hometown fans had never seen him in uniform and were suitably grateful when he was brought in to replace Comiskey in 1895. Although his teams were never able to overcome the redoubtable Orioles or the rising Boston teams, Ewing fielded winners and played himself into retirement before the admiring fans of his native city (Allen, pp. 53–54).

The turn of the century found Cincinnati in the middle of a political era dominated by the figure of George B. Cox. Boss Cox may have been as emblematic of Cincinnati, during this boss-ridden time, as Mayor Kelly and Boss Tweed were appropriate symbols for Chicago and New York. Cox was intelligent, firm but adaptable. He got along well with many of the city's most important families. He loved power and could be brutal when he thought he needed to be. Although his organization grew from headquarters in saloons, Cox was not a particularly "hale fellow well met." He dressed quietly. He built an expensive house in an established neighborhood: well appointed but not a show place. He kept his family out of his public life.

August "Garry" Herrmann was George Cox's alter ego. He was as gregarious and expansive as Cox was withdrawn and sedate. It was the Herrmann side of the Cox regime that was given baseball to enjoy.

The team had been acquired by the Fleischmanns and Cox, none of whom was much interested in running a ball team; so, in 1902, they named Herrmann president, which job he held for a generation, overseeing the team's first World Championship and rising to chairman of the National Commission, whence, in conjunction with the two league presidents, he made professional baseball's decisions. Thus Herrmann put Cincinnati back in the center of the baseball picture, and he did it with a style that many thought especially appropriate:

> He was the personification of Cincinnati culture. To remember him is to remember the outdoor beer gardens and vaudeville, the singing waiters, the foaming steins of beer, the Liederkrantz sandwiches, the belching, guffawing laughter of long-forgotten nights. (Allen, pp. 75–76)

Garry Herrmann may have given new meaning to the word *visible*. Never small, he grew in girth with the years, adding to his sizeable presence with a wardrobe of lavish checks and stripes. He traveled and entertained with an open hand, always finding room for one more at his table. He often made use of a private railroad car, carrying with him supplies of his beloved sausages.

A man of many real achievements, Herrmann sometimes grew impatient with fulsome introductions, interrupting to declare, "Yes, and I am also the champion beer drinker and sausage eater!" His favorite pastime was not public speaking but giving entertainments rich with cheeses, hams, roast chicken, Thuringian blood pudding, liver sausage, and "every type of fermented drink that was known to Bacchus." On one such occasion, given to celebrate the fiftieth year of the National League, Herrmann defied Prohibition to stage a full-blown celebration, all amenities included. John Heydler, the league president and chief speaker, testified that the "big turnout in Cincinnati puts them all in the shade" (Allen, p. 176).

There are shadows over Herrmann's career, including his long association with the Boss, whose reputation began to tarnish while Garry was still in the limelight. He was a principal in the decision to settle the infamous 1919 World Series in five of nine games (instead of the usual four of seven), which format might have made collusion easier to disguise. Yet no black marks have stuck to Herrmann himself. Harry Ellard dedicated *Baseball in Cincinnati* to the Honorable August Herrmann, and *The Sporting News* centennial issue depicted him among the very few administrative leaders to have left their mark on the game. He is known as "the father of the World Series" (Rathgeber, pp. 44–45).

RIGHT: Garry Herrmann, personification of the city's convivial German heritage. (Courtesy Archives and Rare Books Department, University of Cincinnati Libraries) BELOW: This Cincinnati scene was titled "A beer garden on the Rhine." (Courtesy Cincinnati Historical Society)

By the time the National League was congratulating itself on fifty years, Cincinnati had begun to move away from a generation of boss rule. Cox, like other bosses, protected certain neighborhoods and ethnic minorities, but his power did not come from an exercise of pure democracy. Asked by Lincoln Steffens how he could run the city when there was an elected mayor, Cox's famous reply was, "Yes, I have a mayor; but I also have a telephone."

Whether this was a true exchange or a bit of journalistic license is not important. The political boss, especially when long in power, represented corruption. Cox, with his wealth and his telephone, eventually stuck in the public craw. November 8, 1921, the voters passed a referendum in favor of the city manager form of government. Cincinnati embarked on a journey from being reputedly the worst-governed to being reportedly the best-governed city in America.

Extremes of characterization are seldom accurate: just as the city under Cox was probably better governed than some, it would be hard to make a case for any city as being "best." Yet, the voters did their best to go from one extreme to the other. Eventually they enacted a new charter, which gave authority to a council of nine elected through proportional representation: a complex and expensive (and since abandoned) system designed to give minorities their fair weight. The council elected a mayor, whose duties were expected to be mainly ceremonial, and hired a city manager. The boss and his "art of the possible" were replaced by the science of urban management.

Scholars argue about the way in which this transformation affected the city in substance; there can be no doubt that it changed Cincinnati's style. In place of the high-handedness of Cox came a studious, honest series of council members and managers, questing not for personal empires but for a key to the city's future. Eventually the baseball team came to match this new style through leaders such as Powel Crosley, Larry MacPhail, Warren Giles, and particularly Bob Howsam.

The first test for the new Cincinnati was a test that broke the back and spirit of many a metropolis: the Great Depression. The city weathered this worst crisis in the nation's history better than any other major city, partly because of the character of the city, partly because of the new management.

Thanks to the city's diversified industry, unemployment was slow to rise. When business began to fall, employers preferred to cut hours rather than jobs. Cincinnati thus became a city not so much of unemployed as of partly employed. Had the labor force been dominated by a single, strong union, such a plan might have met organized resistance. It did not. One reason was that local workers had always been inclined to put loyalty to church, home, neighborhood, and voluntary associations ahead of blind fealty to the guild (Ross, chap. 1).

No area escaped the Great Depression, and eventually only half of Cincinnati's labor force enjoyed full-time employment. Private charity was unusually responsive to the needy. City and county agencies, compared with federal, handled 70 percent of the burden. On the other hand, because the city had planned ahead, Cincinnati got more than its share of participation in such federal relief programs as the Works Progress Administration.

As if the Depression were not bad enough, the Ohio Valley also suffered, in 1937, a flood that made its predecessors seem like a few splashings alongside the swimming pool. The crisis was met, as usual, by an effective combination of public and private agencies, the schools closing classes while they took in the homeless, and the factories making artesian wells available to a city whose waterworks was underwater.

Depression, compounded by flood, was nearly further compounded by an epic blaze. When a large patch of oily water burst into flame and threatened to spread dramatically, the firefighters extinguished it with special foam nozzles they had received just one week before. The city with America's oldest professional fire department was saved by professional foresight.

The Depression and the flood gave Cincinnati some deep scars. But the new style of government seemed to have proved itself. Under the leadership of former political science professor Clarence Dykstra, the city maintained every important service, fired not a single city employee, and was the only large city not forced to issue its own paper scrip. Political science and planning were affirmed (Silberstein, chap. 19).

In the early 1930s, the Cincinnati Reds were about as low as the Depression-plagued city and nation. The team was chronically last, attendance was correspondingly low, operations showed a debit balance, the team was owned by its creditors, and a move away from the Queen City seemed completely possible. A remedy was at hand, however, and his name was Larry MacPhail, a born promoter and one of the sport's indefatigable innovators.

MacPhail's first need was for an angel, and he was sufficiently persuasive to interest Powel Crosley, prosperous manufacturer of appliances, radios, and—briefly—automobiles. He also owned the leading radio station and the Crosley Broadcasting Company. MacPhail appealed to Crosley's civic spirit, pointing out the likely loss of a franchise from the city where the professional game had its origins. As was usual, MacPhail's sales pitch was successful. In Crosley he found an owner ready with financial support and dedicated to the constructive interaction between the city and the game.

Among MacPhail's many promotional ideas, the most famous was the introduction of night baseball. The game had been played under the lights before, but never in the major leagues. Using Depression conditions as part of his argument—the need for diversion, the commitment of daytime hours to bringing home the scarce bacon—MacPhail won league approval. On May 23, 1935, Paul Derringer beat Joe Bowman and the Phillies under the newly installed lights. The audience numbered 20,422, about ten times as many as might have witnessed that same game in the afternoon. President Roosevelt pressed the switch that turned on the floodlights, and a trend was inaugurated that would eventually make day games during the week virtually obsolete.

It is interesting to note that another great moment in Reds history also took place under the lights. MacPhail left Cincinnati and moved to Brooklyn, where he also had lights installed. There Johnny Vander Meer pitched his second consecutive no-hit game, under the Brooklyn lights.

Some of MacPhail's ideas did not take hold, including the bright red trousers worn by the ballplayers in the early night games. But behind the hype and the novelty was a sound baseball team managed by Bill McKechnie. Built around the dependable arms of Derringer and Bucky Walters, the hitting of Ival Goodman and Frank McCormick, and a fabled "million-dollar infield," the team rose rapidly in the standings. The rise, in fact, exactly paralleled the nation's recovery. In 1937, when the Depression hit its second and most demoralizing trough, the Reds were still last. In 1938, with signs of economic recovery barely visible, the Reds rose to fourth place. In 1939, with war declared in Europe and the American economy saved, the Reds won the pennant, and in 1940, with the economy healthy again, the Reds, victors over Detroit in a hard-fought series, were World Champions.

Radio broadcasts of baseball games were everywhere growing more common. Yet opinion was divided as to whether the broadcasts helped or hurt attendance at the ballpark. It was perhaps inevitable that a man who owned a ball team and a radio station should take the lead in testing the situation. Crosley hired Walter "Red" Barber, a Floridian whose seemingly relaxed descriptions of the game were peppered with southern locutions most people found irresistible. Soon the whole region knew what it meant to be "sittin' in the cat bird's seat." Attendance grew, as did the advertising revenue from the augmented number of broadcasts.

Although Crosley's powerful WLW was not always the voice of the Reds, the regional coverage grew. At the height of the radio age, Cincinnati was the center of a Burger Beer Baseball Network, featuring the former Yankee star Waite Hoyt behind the microphone, selling his product in southern Ohio and Indiana, Kentucky, West Virginia, and northern Tennessee: precisely the area where the Reds began to sell more and more baseball tickets.

Crosley and MacPhail brought not only novelty and victory, but a heightened community involvement. The 1934 scorecard contained Crosley's "message to the fans," which climaxed:

> Cincinnati, the cradle of professional baseball in America, has kept alive the tradition of the famous Championship Red Stockings of 1869. May the Reds of the future deserve the support of Cincinnati fans and preserve the fine traditions of the past.

He not only implied that community loyalty meant support of the ballclub, but he took original means to extend the sport to the city's youth through the establishment of the Knot Hole Club. Based on the cartoon cliché of a truant youngster peering at a game through a hole in a wooden fence, the Knot Hole Club reversed this image by insisting on a signed pledge from every youngster who wished to participate:

> I will not at any time skip school.
> I will attend no game against the wishes of my parents.
> I will practice clean speech, clean sport and clean habits.
> I will try by attendance, deportment and effort at school or work to prove
>   my worthiness to membership in the club.

Giving out free tickets to the young folks created a habit of loyalty. Giving the authority to hand out the cherished Knot Hole cards to school teachers provided a way to enforce authority that pleased another, older segment of the community.

The Knot Hole Club had a song and a radio program. Most important, it provided leagues for organized play in every neighborhood, culminating in public playoffs at Deer Creek park, just outside the downtown area, for the championship of the city in several age brackets. The idea of neighborhood leagues was not new and has, by now, grown far beyond the ambitious Knot Hole program. The Reds of Powel Crosley and Larry

MacPhail not only gave this concept a shot in the arm during the depths of the Depression when it was sorely needed, but they also connected the youngsters' earliest baseball experiences with the benevolence of the hometown Reds.

The Cincinnati past provides a clear prologue to the triumphs of the 1960s and '70s. Even a few episodes suggest the careful concern for the development of a balanced, prosperous community through the use of technology. They show that the search for progess without disorder is not a modern invention. Putting aside the flamboyance and glitter of other cities, Cincinnatians have long shown their willingness to be seen as a place where hard work and family come first but where the threat of dullness is relieved by music and sport, beer and sausage, and the frequently recurring festivals. One thread that has linked these attitudes and values has been the game of baseball and the city's professsional team.

Chapter Two.....
SETTING THE STAGE

On the 1970 National League schedule, June 30 looks like many another summer day. On a full card, the Cincinnati entry was hosting the Atlanta Braves with nothing vital at stake. Locally, however, it was anything but an ordinary day. It punctuated a long history of infatuation with the national game. It was a landmark in an eighty-year-long legacy of planning, capping the surge of a downtown renaissance. It represented the achievement of a community where public works were often buttressed by private and corporate voluntarism. It was opening day at the Cincinnati Riverfront Stadium.

The 51,051 spectators were offered an "Opening Souvenir Magazine," which, along with pages of facts and boasts about the new facility, contained a capsule review of the struggle to commit the city to a modern arena placed conspicuously between the broad Ohio and the historic downtown business district. The author cited an editorial published December 1, 1965, by the *Cincinnati Enquirer:*

> We confidently predict that once the new stadium has become a reality, its greatest significance will not be as a remarkable new facility (although it clearly will be that) but as a monument to a new spirit in the Queen City—a spirit that admits no obstacles, a spirit that enlists the best that Cincinnatians have to offer, a spirit that gets things done.

To appreciate this conjunction of professional sport and urban renewal, it is necessary to recall elements from the past.

The compulsion to plan may run in the Cincinnati bloodstream, as evidenced by the railroad to the south, the notable bridges, and the pioneering public Parks Commission appointed in 1906. There is little doubt that this inherent tendency was enormously amplified by the happy accident that made the Queen City the home of Alfred Bettman, considered by many the "father of modern urban planning." Bettman was a Harvard-educated lawyer, nationally famous as a prosecutor in criminal courts, and as a special assistant to Attorney General A. Mitchell Palmer during World War I. His law practice furnished him the wherewithal to pursue an avocation that eventually made him a national leader in urban and regional planning in America during the years betweem the two world wars (Gerckens, p. 144).

No one gets very far in planning without confronting the realities of urban politics. Bettman's initiation came in 1909 with a two-year term as Hamilton County (Cincinnati) prosecutor and escalated in 1911 with the unlikely victory of Henry T. Hunt as mayor of the city. Hunt defeated the Cox machine candidate and brought with him Bettman as city solicitor. In their brief term in office, Hunt and Bettman were forced to confront the malfeasance and nonfeasance of the machine and to propose ways of reversing the city's staggering debts and diminishing services: paths that would not be followed until the next decade.

Alfred Bettman's close-quarter clash with corruption led him to see planning as synonymous with political reform. As his ideas led him steadily to regional and national prominence in planning councils and in the drafting of planning legislation, he inevitably pushed his home town to the front of this new wave. Thus the growth of the antimachine charter movement and the growth of planning worked hand in hand, united by the figure of Bettman.

Foreshadowing some of the events leading to the building of Riverfront were the early struggles to create planning authority. The first authorization of such activity, typically, included no cash appropriations. Private gifts were therefore solicited, including donations through the Community Chest, and the essential $100,000 was raised in amounts ranging from $1 to $15,000. The work toward the 1925 City Plan was underway, and Cincinnati became "the first large city to devise a long-range programming procedure definitely related to a comprehensive city plan" (Scott, p. 253).

Typical of a city that consistently stresses professionalism was Bettman's insistence, when he took his seat on the Cincinnati City Planning Commission in 1926, that financial support become a regular budgetary item. This led to the hiring of the nation's first full-time municipally employed professional planner.

Although the 1925 master plan was soon outdated, it was succeeded by the fifteen-volume Plan of 1948, whose frontispiece is a portrait of Alfred Bettman (1873–1945) inscribed:

> As long as Cincinnatians love their city and strive for its future greatness; as long as they remain eager to make it the best place in all the world in which to live, the spirit and work of Alfred Bettman . . . will live on.

Alfred Bettman, father of modern city planning. (City Planning Commission, *The Cincinnati Metropolitan Master Plan and the Official City Plan, Adopted November 22, 1948*)

Bettman did not live to see the largest ramifications of his tireless pioneering, but he did enjoy a double vindication in 1924 and '25, when the two parts of the City Plan were approved. At that same time, charter government and the city-manager system were adopted and confirmed by an election which left only three members of the old machine to face twice that number of reform-minded councilmen.

Thus, in "two short years," writes Laurence Gerckens, the city was changed from the "worst governed" to the "best governed" as a result of "Bettman's concepts of city planning as reform and municipal economy, his implementation of Hunt's concepts of participatory democracy and capital planning, and the Charterite political revolution" (Gerckens, p. 133).

The legacy of Bettman and the planners affected the setting for professional baseball in a number of ways: by demonstrating that a city was not just a political entity but part of a region whose identity radiated from the urban center along a number of vectors; by showing that development meant cooperation between the governments of the communities, the counties, and the states; by locating capital investment priorities which would not only guide the public treasury but would also establish a matrix for private investments. The expressway system is the most visible feature of the Plan of 1948. The "most astonishing" aspect of this motor network, writes Iola Silberstein, is that it is virtually complete (Silberstein, p. 237).

The Plan of 1948 identified a complex of highways called the Third Street Distributor. This is where the interstate system and the commuter network would either merge in a thrilling vehicular confluence, or become the Midwest's worst bottleneck. This arterial system, in the plan, marked the northern boundary of an area called Riverfront. Along the river, adjacent to the Suspension Bridge, was a large shape labeled "stadium" and showing a fan-shaped playing area containing the familiar interior diamond. Relating reclamation, sport, and profit, the planners asserted:

> Adequate facilities to accommodate conventions and major sports events will draw large numbers of people from out of town. The Cincinnati Convention and Visitors Bureau estimates Cincinnati has lost $1,000,000 a year for lack of facilities for major sports events. (p. 149)

EPR: "When talking about the modern city, the Plan of '48 is as good a place as any to start. There was an earlier master plan, of course, produced in the 1920s. All of this was of course before I came on the

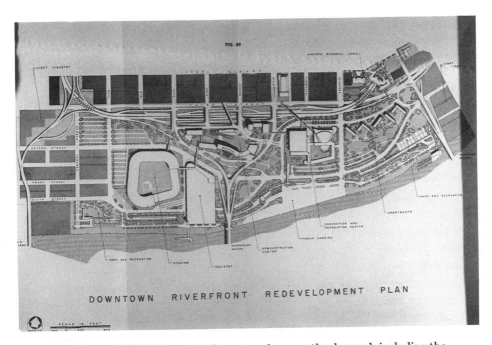

DOWNTOWN RIVERFRONT REDEVELOPMENT PLAN

The "Plan of 1948." Many details were subsequently changed, including the location of home plate, but the basic elements were realized: the highway distributor and the new stadium's site between the central business district and the river. (City Planning Commission, *The Cincinnati Metropolitan Master Plan and the Official City Plan, Adopted November 22, 1948*) scene politically. But by the time I arrived the city already had quite a tradition of planning: it had an excellent planning department with a first-rate planning staff; and I think it served the city well."

Q: "But the Plan of '48 did not lead directly to solving the problems of downtown?"

EPR: "That's right. The real planning for downtown took place in the sixties. We were having a great debate about what to do to revitalize downtown Cincinnati. It was becoming a political football. No progress. Until eventually a group was put together including professional planners, business leaders, and three councilmen. This group hired Arch Rogers for his experience in replanning downtown Baltimore. Using this experience Rogers very skillfully built the support of that nonpartisan committee into a plan for downtown: the elevated pedestrian walkways, the reconstruction of Fountain Square—the things that eventually led to the inner-city renaissance.

"But this plan did not include the riverfront. We were only able to build this area into the city pattern with the aid of federal grants. Federal funds were used to acquire substandard lands which were then written down in value and sold for new development. In about 1962 the city passed a bond issue for a total of $16 million that led to the building of a convention center and the further development of the riverfront. In 1967 these features were added to the downtown and became important in the process of redevelopment.

"The stadium itself, however, did not become an issue until 1966–67. It is important to note that by the time the stadium issue came up, we had an accepted plan for the downtown in place and were working on it. Therefore, when the stadium consultant came back with a report of four possible sites, everyone on the city council favored the riverfront, the only site adjacent to downtown."

Q: "The council was unanimous?"

EPR: "On where it should be if it were built. The Democratic Party members opposed the idea of building a stadium at all: opposed it from beginning to end. But there was no question on the council that, if a stadium were to be built, it would be between downtown and the river."

(Gene Ruehlmann is here recalling a sequence of events in bare outline. A full and enlightening story is told by the city's current director of utilities, Joe Rochford, in an unpublished paper titled "The Games Cities Play: Cincinnati's Decision to Build Riverfront Stadium." Part of Rochford's thesis is that the key decisions were made in 1966; he supports the universal view of Ruehlmann as the central figure. In the summer of 1987, a study published by the Heartland Institute insisted that investments by cities in professional sports stadiums did not justify themselves economically. This position got a strong rebuttal from Rob Daumeyer's article in the *Cincinnati Business Courier* of August 6–12, 1987. Joe Rochford reported that the city got a direct return of $4 million in 1985 on their annual rent of $2.6 million. From an urban planning perspective, see also Scott, pp. 570ff.).

Locating the stadium was one of many issues that brought up the question of region. Many followers of Cincinnati sports assume that the Reds are essentially an Ohio team. They note the prominence of the Dayton sportswriters. They watch the cars stream into town from Xenia and Portsmouth. They read such polls as the one conducted by the University of Cincinnati in 1984 that found the Reds the favorite team of 82 percent of southwestern Ohioans. More astounding, even in the northwest part of the state, where loyalties ought to be divided between Cleveland and Detroit, the Reds still claimed the fealty of 17 percent of the fans, only one point below the Indians. Two of the sites recommended by the consultant—Maketewah and Blue Ash—were strategically placed between the interstate highways that led in from Dayton and Columbus. If the Buckeye fans could be spared a trip through the congested city, and the parking problems of the desolate West End, who knew how many would fill the seats? Thus reasoned Reds owner Bill DeWitt, who favored Blue Ash, and many agreed.

The people who market Reds baseball had long ago discovered consumers along other compass headings. The Burger Beer Baseball Network of the 1930s through the 1950s was aimed, like the city's railroad, at the South. Gordon Coleman, once a hard-hitting first baseman for the Reds, recalls that in 1968 Bob Howsam created the Reds Speakers Bureau and made him director. "Since then I have averaged a thousand miles a week, bringing highlight films and players, talking myself to people all around this part of the country. I can tell you exactly where Reds country ends. Draw a line south from Indianapolis to Louisville, for example. Everything west of that line belongs to the Cardinals.

"Gradually we made the speaking trips more regular and organized what is now called the Red Caravan: a bus trip with overnight stops and scheduled appearances. It goes to Dayton, Columbus, Indianapolis, Lexington, Louisville, and Huntington, West Virginia. In all these places—and in between—the Reds are known as 'our team.' "

Marketing experience showed that the interest in the ball team was not limited by state boundaries. Rather, Reds country was more circular with the city in the center. As differentiated from the proposed sites north of the city, the riverfront location—so long as the Third Street Distributor worked—was convenient to the major highways coming from all points of the compass.

The advantageous placing of a new stadium was one part of a battle just to keep the franchise.

EPR: "Losing the ball team was a real possibility. Across the country were cities aggressively searching for a franchise, and here we were, stuck with dowdy old Crosley Field, seating only 28,000 and in a part of town where you paid a kid to watch your car and still worried about slashed tires. So we turned our attention to the impact of baseball on other cities: places like Milwaukee that had attracted a franchise then lost it; Philadelphia and Pittsburgh that were building modern stadiums. We visited Anaheim, Houston, and Chavez Ravine. We knew what Busch Stadium had done for St. Louis.

"The report that resulted from these visits and studies showed that there was just no question: a major-league franchise was a significant economic benefit to a metropolitan area. Our problem became, then, what do we have to do to get a stadium? And we soon became convinced that baseball alone was not enough to provide the financial base. We would also need a professional football franchise. And this is where Governor James A. Rhodes came in. He came down to a Chamber of Commerce luncheon and told them that if we would build the stadium he would make sure we got a new franchise headed by Paul Brown, who had brought so much success to Cleveland. This really lit a spark.

"There were plenty of problems, though. Bill DeWitt not only favored Blue Ash, he actively disliked the riverfront site. He feared flooding. He also opposed the configuration necessary for a two-sport stadium, wanting a ballpark where the stands followed closely and symmetrically along the foul lines. When we found out the size of the bond issue needed to build this stadium, we felt we should have a forty-year lease from the Reds ownership. DeWitt refused.

" 'Would you be willing to sell the team so we can get on with this project?' I asked him. After due deliberation he agreed with certain conditions. The price was no problem. A fair price was agreed upon. But DeWitt insisted that the buyers be local people and that they be forced to sign the same lease that had been offered to him."

The manner in which this crisis was met is somewhat reminiscent of the time when eight "prominent citizens" arose to pay the debts of the 1887

Reds when the owner, meatpacker Josiah Keck, grew tired of a losing team and walked away from the whole thing. In that instance the issue was the disgrace that might tarnish the city's name should the team default on its sporting commitments. In 1966 it was the threat of losing a cherished possession: possibly an economic asset but most certainly the emotional heart of the community for ninety-seven years.

Some dozen individuals, all but one a Cincinnati resident and most of them recognized civic leaders, organized themselves as "617, Inc." and raised a reported $7 million to buy the team from DeWitt. (The name of the corporation derived from the street address of the *Cincinnati Enquirer*, whose president and publisher, Francis Dale, became president of the Reds.) As subsequent events were to prove, 617 had no interest in owning a baseball team. They pitched in to move the city off a sharp place, caught as it was between an owner who refused to sign a lease and a stadium that could not be financed without such a commitment.

Q: "Wasn't this a red-letter day in the history of civic spirit?"

EPR: "Yes it was, but I can give you plenty more examples of the way in which prompt and generous action by private citizens saved the stadium from a fatal sidetrack. For instance, when the idea of the stadium was proposed, we needed a feasibility study and had no funds available. Two individuals, David Frisch and Hulbert Taft, gave $25,000 each to provide the sum needed for the study.

"Subsequently, when the idea of the stadium was gaining support but still lacked council willingness to spend money, I went to the Chamber of Commerce, which in ten days raised $250,000 for the preliminary architectural work. You understand that there were time pressures. The professional football leagues had let us know that if we didn't have a stadium by 1970 we could forget the football franchise; so we had to keep things moving. But can you imagine private individuals and businesses risking that much money? To be sure, the money would be refunded if the stadium went ahead. But if it did not—and the outcome was by no means assured—this money would become a simple donation to the city."

Q: "That is an impressive case of what you call 'corporate citizenship.' What were the motives? Were these donors simply sports-minded, or were they equally interested in the downtown renaissance?"

EPR: "First, contributions came from many private citizens as well as corporations. As to the motives, I can't say yes or no to that. But I can tell you that by this time there was momentum building toward doing something concrete for the old business district. I can also tell you that if you ask the merchants in downtown Cincinnati what their businesses were like before and after the opening of the stadium, they will tell you it was the most important event in the city's recent history.

"You notice the way the stadium is laid out, with its adjacent parking areas. There are about 4,500 new parking places. Now that is not enough for a stadium that holds 55,000 people. There are another 18,000 parking places north of the expressway in the downtown area. People park there and walk down over the pedestrian bridges. Along the way to or from the stadium they may well stop for a beer or a sandwich, a newspaper or a souvenir. Furthermore, this keeps the automobile traffic from centering at the stadium itself and avoids potential massive traffic jams.

"The city has profited, as our studies showed it would, from professional sports franchises located adjacent to the downtown business center. Our consultant was also right about the traffic advantages. It is convenient to the interstate highways from *all* points of the compass. The 'distributor' design handles this with very little strain. It works."

Q: "But what about Bill DeWitt's fears? Will Riverfront Stadium, like a huge circular tub, go floating one day down the swollen Ohio?"

EPR: "You remember the Great Flood of 1937 from our high school days, and you remember that it reached eighty feet—or almost eighty feet. The stadium is designed to be usable at eighty feet—a level we'll never see again because of the dams and flood control upstream. Such were not in place in '37."

Q to Bob Howsam: "Were you in on the discussion of where to build a stadium?"

HOWSAM: "No, I was not. But in my opinion, if it had not been for Mayor Gene Ruehlmann, Cincinnati never would have had a stadium. I mean even after there was a degree of commitment, because there was a group on the council—Democrats and Charter—who were fighting the idea of building a stadium anywhere.

"There was a fight about where to put the stadium, and, although I was not directly involved, I was surely in favor of the downtown site. This was because of my experience at St. Louis, where I had seen what such a setting could do for a city and for the team. I saw the downtown site as *ideal*.

"There is no doubt in my mind that the building of Riverfront Stadium is the *key*, in my estimation, to that area of the city coming back and to Cincinnati being what it is today. And without Gene they never would have had it, even after contracts were signed and all that.

"I did make some changes in Riverfront before it was completed.

TOP: Crosley Field during the 1937 flood. (Courtesy *Cincinnati Enquirer*)
BOTTOM: The new stadium, just under construction, flooded by the rising
Ohio. (Courtesy Riverfront Stadium Management)

DeWitt had wanted the offices on the upper floors; I thought they should be down in the guts of the building where you could see what was going on. Then I had them remove the Plexiglas barrier they had intended to put behind home plate. This is a bad idea. I had seen it at the old Seals stadium in San Francisco. It blocks out the sound, which is a big part of fan enjoyment.

"You want people to be fans, who cheer for the team that represents their city, but you also want them involved in the game. If you block out the sound, you remove a lot of the excitement.

"Then you want to do everything you can to promote second-guessing. We made a mistake in St. Louis by putting the bullpens out of sight. As soon as the fans see a pitcher warming up, they all become instant managers. And this is good. That is why the designated hitter is a bad idea: it removes so many possibilities for second-guessing, and it has made American League baseball—whether they like it or not—a duller game.

"Also, I fought hard to get permission for artificial turf covering the whole field of play—except of course for the sliding areas around the bases. At that time, although there were artificial turf stadiums, they all had dirt infields as with the natural grass field. At first I was given permission to have such a field for only a year. Then I won approval to keep it, and now several fields are made that way.

"There are really only a few things you have to do well in order to have a successful franchise. Some of them have to do with the stadium itself: a design that will involve the fan in the game as fully as possible. Then there is the look of the place and its condition. It should be clean and attractive. If you expect people to spend three or four hours there, they should feel as comfortable as in their own homes. But since the stadium is also a setting, the field of play should be as attractive as a well set stage.

"So the artificial turf comes in for a number of reasons. It always looks good. It doesn't need cutting and trimming and watering. It is a pleasing color, allowing a contrast with the white of the ball, a contrast that allows the eye to follow the ball wherever it goes against the turf.

"Most important, turf allows the game to be played the way it was meant to be played. Why should we take and work so hard to get a perfect dirt-and-grass infield? We can come much closer with the artificial turf. Therefore, chance has less to do with the outcome. Home teams can't tamper with the surface and give themselves an unfair advantage. The fast bounces on the carpet, coupled with good arms in the outfield, make for close plays on baserunners: excitement. And of course this is what the fans love.

"The whole ballpark should be an enjoyable place, a place where you will take your whole family. I have done everything I could think of to contribute to this. I tried to serve the best hotdog possible: pure beef. They were made for us by Wilson, and they were excellent. But they contained no meal and they were tougher to chew, an the fans didn't like them. But I was trying for something so delicious that you would finish one and immediately go for another."

Q: "Is it true that you wanted the place to smell like a bakery? The one smell that makes everybody happy and hungry?"

HOWSAM: "Yes. That is exactly what I wanted. I had some involvement with the University of Denver, and their business school was conducting some experiments in novel aids to business. So I asked them to see if they couldn't make us a spray or something that we could use to give that nice fragrance to the ballpark. What could be better? But unfortunately they couldn't do it."

Before there could be hotdogs and aromas there had to be a stadium, and people had to know what to call it. For a long period in the late 1960s naming the new ballpark was a favorite pastime. The evening newspaper distributed coupons, of which 31,000 were submitted offering up more than 3,000 different names. A radio and television station staged a contest, then announced the seven most popular names. The nominations showed what was on the public mind at this time and how they thought of their city.

There was a small but persistent suggestion that the name of Ohio's astronaut, Neil Armstrong, be honored. More common suggestions, in ascending order of popularity, were those of Senator Taft, President Eisenhower, Governor Rhodes, Powel Crosley (who had given his name to the old field), and Fred Hutchinson, an inspirational manager who had died prematurely.

The polls seemed to show a media-related class bias. Those who phoned in votes to the radio and television station made Regal Stadium their second choice; those who wrote, favored this name in third place. For those who sent coupons to the newspaper, however, regality had no appeal whatsoever, while the People's Stadium finished fifth.

A public-relations expert, in a letter to the county commissioners, toyed with such names as Cincinnatus, Riverbank, Downtown, and even Red Bengal before coming down for a very popular choice (first, second, and third in the three media polls), Queen City Stadium. Residents of the area still thought of their city as the "Queen City of the West" and didn't care who knew it. At least, they thought, it would represent the best in the state, and they suggested, with regularity, such names as Buckeye Bowl and Ohio Stadium.

Five weeks before the stadium opened, it still lacked an official name. The man who did the most to make it all happen took the issue directly to the city council in a letter dated May 13, 1970. "It is my opinion that the Citizens of Greater Cincinnati have already named the stadium. It is 'The Cincinnati Riverfront Stadium.' " The polls roughly confirmed what His Honor, Mayor Ruehlmann, had announced, ranking it first, second, and fifth in the three surveys. It seems to have been a popular choice. To historians and planners it is a comforting name, harking back to the famous Plan of 1948, which both designated the Riverfront area and drew in a dominant feature marked "stadium."

To the observer of the American scene, Riverfront Stadium is just one of a series of roughly circular, multiuse public arenas, as flat in their similarities as they are interesting in their differences. There is no community, however, which has invested in a sports facility so much of its historic character and so much of its future hopes. Historians of planning date Cincinnati's entry into the modern era from the 1906 formation of a Parks Commission and the appropriation of $15,000 to execute its plans (Gerckens, p. 122; Vexler, p. 47). This action signaled the city's commitment, early in the century, to a public investment in the preservation of open spaces as well as the importance of sport and recreation.

The stadium illustrates many of the principles of the city's pioneer planner, Alfred Bettman. Bettman, who kept pushing planning outward from its political boundaries, would have been delighted to see a facility situated with multistate access in mind. As one who defined the city's role as a constructive example of capital investment, Bettman would have applauded the economic benefits as well as the evident respect for intangibles called civic pride.

As a man who remembered the days when the Cincinnati basin defined a true "walking city," Alfred Bettman would have loved the proximity of the ballpark to the historic center of this old river city; he would have given particularly hearty applause to the pedestrian bridges that made the joys of walking actual. The planners of 1948 recognized their master plan as Bettman's most explicit local legacy: hence their moving dedication. To them, and to the subsequent advocates of downtown renewal, Riverfront Stadium was essential. It anchored their plans and hopes along two important axes, offering a congenial southern boundary to the business district while dramatizing the north-south axis that included the renovated Fountain Square, the Public Library, the Convention Center, and the other central features of a hollow urban heart brought back to its vital beat.

It is not possible to know the full history of any public event in a modern, complex community. Too much takes place at private lunches at the Queen City Club, during bantering phone calls made ostensibly to confirm a tee-off time, or simply in a few words exchanged while walking along Fourth Street between Walnut and Vine. All older cities have their established families dedicated to anonymity as well as to the long-term welfare of the community. George Anderson and John Bench, among the members of the baseball community, were struck by the relatively small number of these powerful local families, as well as by how well they knew each other and—in certain settings—worked together.

Keeping the Reds in Cincinnati and getting them a suitable place to play has, at one time or another, involved many of these families, as is only fractionally exemplified by the 617 group and the donors to the Chamber of Commerce campaign to raise architects' fees. Yet these often unseen forces would be completely frustrated without visible, capable public leadership. What makes Cincinnati interesting, in the present context, is the profound positive coincidence of two public careers coming together at the same time and in the same place. One of these careers is that of Eugene Peter Ruehlmann, a native Cincinnatian first elected to the city council in 1959. His perceptions have helped shape this exploration of city and sport. Everyone's choice as the key figure in bringing Riverfront Stadium to pass, he was first elected mayor in 1967.

Gene Ruehlmann, directly involved with the city, could not help becoming a part of the development of professional sports. Born and raised in the city's sports-rich Western Hills, Gene graduated from the University of Cincinnati, then from Harvard Law School, becoming a practicing attorney. Along the way he married the lovely Virginia Juergens; they have eight children, including several who have followed into law.

Since 1959, when he was first elected a Republican member of the city council, Eugene Peter Ruehlmann has been clearly among those carrying the city's destiny. This public trust grew with each of the five reelections, with the four years as vice mayor and culminating in two terms as mayor, 1967–71, the crucial years for downtown renewal and for Riverfront. Among the many indications of accepted responsibilities in Gene's public history are three which happen to be listed consecutively in his biographical summary and which fairly symbolize the nature of his commitment: founder of the Mayor's Housing Coordinating Committee; cosponsor of the Citizens' Committee to Improve Local Government and of the Mayor's

Prayer Breakfast. Together they suggest Gene's ingenuity in bringing together the forces of religion, business, and politics to create that stable and progressive context through which a community shows its best mid-western face.

Everyone agrees that without Gene Ruehlmann there would be no Riverfront. It is at least a consensus that Ruehlmann's achievements go even further; that Riverfront is a metaphor representing the accomplishments of one of the most effective leaders in the Queen City's two-hundred-year history.

The year Gene Ruehlmann was first elected mayor, 1967, was the year Bob Howsam was hired as general manager of the ballclub. This coincidence made memorable the decade of the 1970s in Cincinnati. To Ruehlmann's political persistence was added the imagination necessary to make the new stadium an effective canvas. The big investment by the Ohio would have fallen far short of its potential without the development of a championship team—one that dominated the 1970s as few teams have ever prevailed over a ten-year period—and a team that responded to the special traits of the river city and its regional setting.

Bob Howsam was born in Denver, Colorado, on the twenty-eighth of February, 1918. He attended the University of Colorado, served in the navy, and by the age of thirty had become president of the Denver baseball club in the American Association. Those who know Howsam well identify two central influences on his professional life. One was Edwin C. Johnson, who served both as governor of Colorado and as United States senator. Howsam married Johnson's daughter, Janet, thus becoming part of the family of this outstanding political leader, a man who specialized in mastering the art of the possible. Howsam's skill in dealing with business and political leaders in Cincinnati can surely be attributed to the wisdom acquired at the feet of his father-in-law.

The second great influence was Branch Rickey—the source of enough baseball wisdom to dwarf any room full of pundits. The association did not begin well, according to Rickey's biographer. The elder Rickey, Howsam had heard, was referred to as Branch while his son, Branch Jr., was called Twig. It was thus that Bob Howsam addressed the two of them as they gathered to discuss the formation of a new "Western League." If this story is true, it must have been an embarrassing moment indeed, since the elder Rickey was and is consistently called *Mr.* Rickey by one and all. In spite of this awkward introduction, the relationship continued and deepened. Howsam calls Mr. Rickey "one of the greatest baseball men of all time and the best judge of baseball talent I ever knew."

It was Branch Rickey who recommended Howsam to August Busch when Busch insisted on firing Bing Devine.

The appointment of Robert Howsam as general manager of the St. Louis Cardinals in 1964 led to his eventual destiny on the Ohio. Here the general manager acquired direct experience in moving a ballclub from an older stadium to a new one, by a river, and adjacent to a historic but eroded business district. Here Howsam showed his fine trading hand, particularly in acquiring Orlando Cepeda. Here he put together championship teams playing on artificial turf. Most important, in a city very much like Cincinnati, Howsam showed that he understood the subtleties of marketing a sports product in Mid-America.

In spite of his many successes with the Cardinals, Howsam was never given a free hand. Caught in a factionalism he had no part in creating, Howsam was also at the mercy of a sometimes unpredictable owner. Thus he was more than ready to talk to the delegates of the new Reds owners when they came knocking late in 1966. "I wanted the chance to really run things. I thought I had proved I knew how to do it."

By the time he came to Cincinnati in 1967, Bob Howsam had indeed learned a lot of things, whether in Denver or St. Louis, whether in trying to launch a new baseball league or a new football team, whether from a United States senator or from the patriarch of modern baseball. He knew that being a millionaire did not necessarily incline one to loose purse-strings, and that he had better find a way to start the turnstiles spinning at old Crosley Field before asking the owners to pay the big tab necessary to rejuvenate the scouting staff and the farm system. He knew that you don't sell baseball in the Midwest the way you might sell, for example, skiing in Aspen. He knew that baseball was first and foremost a business and that businesses do not succeed without attention to administrative detail and without offering a distinctive and appealing product.

Sooner or later, it all comes down to winning. What happens on the field is basic and indispensable; but the team can also be a metaphor for the whole organization.

HOWSAM: "There was one man who may've been even better than Mr. Rickey when it came to balancing a ballclub. That was George Weiss of the Yankees. Certainly he and Mr. Rickey were the two best, and I had the privilege of being associated with both of them: Weiss when I was president of a Yankee farm club. You remember those acquisitions he used to make at the end of the season? At a time when the Yankees seemed unbeatable, but where he saw a flaw—the need for a right-handed pinch-hitter or a left-handed reliever? And how those acquisitions of his always seemed to loom large in the Series? Mr. Rickey did the same thing through his farm systems; George Weiss did it more spectacularly through those selective trades and purchases."

The purpose of balance is not simply to provide the abilities necessary to make more runs than the opposition. There needs to be a balance of temperaments and personal goals so that a roster of players can truly become a team.

HOWSAM: "You know a team, regardless of its record, always seems to think it is doing as well as it can. With the right balance of skills and personalities, however, you can create the kind of interaction that makes for a true team spirit. Real professionalism. Inner competitiveness, but also harmony. With this a team may seem to be playing over its head, but it is really just living up to its true potential. And that can be enough."

Howsam was more than a shrewd trader, a resourceful marketer, and an experienced entrepreneur. His combination of abilities put a team on the field that played to its full potential. This spirit also involved the entire Reds system, from owners to scouts and clubhousemen. In a way that is not easy to describe, this synergy seemed to flow through the city and its surrounding region, making the team a symbol for Redland as it liked to see itself and as it liked to be seen.

HOWSAM: "You know when I went home to spend Christmas with my family in Colorado in 1966, I had just taken the Cincinnati job. "Where is it?' they asked. Well, before too long, nobody had to ask where Cincinnati was. In the business community Procter & Gamble had put the city on the map, but business doesn't touch people the way sport does. I have to be careful what I say here because I had a part in it, but I honestly think that the Reds of the seventies played a major role in showing the world—the baseball world, at least—what a fine and important city this is."

In 1973 the Greater Cincinnati Convention and Visitors Bureau presented Robert L. Howsam with a handsome plaque, hung conspicuously in his Glenwood Springs den, that proclaims him the leading ambassador for Cincinnati. Also in 1973 *The Sporting News* named Howsam Baseball Executive of the Year.

The opening of Riverfront Stadium, on June 30, furnished a kind of negative victory. It showed the doubters that a stadium could be built and, if incomplete, could serve its purpose. The baseball team would not drift into oblivion with aging Crosley Field, and the demands of the football league would be met.

Difficulties still remained. Their magnitude can be gathered from a report to the city council dated August 5, 1970, when the ballpark had been in use for over a month. During July, reported the city manager, the Reds had played their full schedule; there had been a two-day open house as well as the All Star Game. During this time, work continued on such prominent features as the scoreboard and the sound system which, though incomplete, were "placed in operation for each event." Other incomplete items included escalators, stairs, locker rooms, offices, restrooms, ticket booths, lighting, press facilities, and painting, not to mention those features necessary for transforming the stadium from baseball to football. Pedestrian traffic, concluded the report, had been facilitated by using the bus-taxi bridge and by placing a "movable auxiliary stairway" at the north end of the pedestrian bridge.

Psychologically, the stadium opened not on June 30 but on July 14, when the All Star Game put it on display for the nation. It was a clearly affirmative occasion. The Queen City hosted the best of the major leagues in the most modern (so modern it was not even finished!) of stadiums. They showed the world the first complete artificial turf covering as well as the most convenient access to a center city. They sold beer and German sausages. The National League won again—as it had every time the game was played in the Queen City. The victory came on the relentless dash of the city's own hardworking German-American: the man they call Charlie Hustle.

Chapter Three.....
THE IMAGE
Clean and Traditional

Q: "Who was responsible for the Reds' three esses: black shoes, high socks, and clean shaves?

SPARKY: "Howsam, all Howsam. To me it was the greatest thing he ever did. His greatest thing was that he never wavered on that. Because, if you remember, we were in an era of social change. Finley was giving $300 for guys to wear mustaches. The long hair had come in. Trousers down to the ankles with nothing but all-white sanitary showing behind and looking like a Sunday semipro team. That's what they looked like to me. Through all these changes, and there were plenty of them, Howsam never wavered. He did a lot of great things in his career, but this to me was the greatest.

"He had a picture of Woody Woodward taken showing the proper way to wear the uniform. That was always there. We have gone through at least three eras in the last fifteen years, and still the Reds to me are the only ones that look like a major-league team. They look major-league. And they never change. And that to me is the best legacy Howsam left our game."

Q: "Who did he do it for? Was it to appeal to a certain kind of fan? Or was it for himself?"

SPARKY: "He did it for himself because he believed that this was all part of a Broadway production. He never interfered with me on baseball questions: how to play the game on the field. He never pretended to special knowledge about that. But find a batting helmet with a chip out of it? Or a uniform dirty at game time? We would really hear about that. I got more memos in red—because he always wrote in red ink because it was the Reds—fussing about things that were not up to the standards of a Broadway show!"

A story confirmed by both Sparky and Howsam concerns the batting helmet of Pete Rose. Pete had chalked his number 14 on the back to make it easier to locate (such numbers are now stenciled on). It was a road game and Howsam was not present, but as the TV camera swept the dugout the offending helmet was visible. Howsam was immediately on the phone, connected to the dugout, and presto: the chalk mark disappeared. Sportswriter Hal McCoy, who reported the helmet story, depicts an even more memorable scene epitomizing the Howsam Reds. It features a clubhouse attendant patiently rubbing black shoe polish into all the stripes and wings and other logos with which the manufacturers have adorned the players' shoes. Once they leave the clubhouse, these once-flashy shoes will be uniformly black (McCoy, p. 25).

HOWSAM: "You want to know why the shoes are black? One reason is because white shoes exaggerate the length of the foot. They are like the shoes circus clowns wear. A team in light-colored shoes always looked to me like a Sunday School softball team.

"More important is that the center of the game is the ball. The ball is white. As the white ball goes skimming along the playing surface, white shoes distract the eye. Black is the ultimate contrast: it sets off the white. It dramatizes the game and keeps the attention on the ball, where it belongs."

SPARKY: "I'd say Howsam maintained the great standards of the game, what it had been. I've seen many men since Howsam tear it down."

What exactly was this look that Howsam insisted on and which became associated with the Big Red Machine of the 1970s? It did not deliberately ape the old-time uniforms made of heavy flannel and sporting high collars and gothic lettering. In 1972 the Reds joined the many other teams that had shifted to double-knit man-made fabric. It was lighter, cooler, gave with body movements, and was—a definite plus for Howsam—easier to clean. The belt, with its interlocking loops that kept shirt and trousers together, had given way to snaps. No buttons anywhere. The discarded shirts, unadorned at the collar and sleeves, were replaced by slipover tops with red borders. The uniform itself is hard to distinguish from others, particularly that of the St. Louis Cardinals. The one traditional feature was the all-black shoes worn while other teams were adopting colors to match their uniforms.

STOWE: "You see, the Reds were one of the first teams to use the new athletic shoes and to pick a color to match the uniform. They were all using Adidas red shoes with white stripes. But Jim Maloney and Tony Cloninger (this was in '69) found they couldn't pitch in those shoes, so they had to wear their old black shoes. At which point Mr. Howsam says, 'Oh, no. Everyone has to have the same color shoes. Two black, everybody black.' And from then on it was all black shoes for everyone.

"To tell the truth, I kind of like the black or the black with white striping. The contrast is good. But look at these red shoes they're wearing now ('87). They are different shades, see? No two of 'em the same color really."

The distinctiveness was in the way the uniform was worn. In the face of a general tendency to wear the trousers lower and lower on the calves, the Reds insisted that baseball's knickers were meant to end just below the knee. While other teams lengthened the trousers, they also stretched the stirrups of the colorful team sox until the sock itself disappeared, leaving only the thin stirrup against the background of the white "sanitary" or sweat sock that had always been worn beneath the dyed hose to prevent infection.

Ironically, it was the "counterculture" look that was heading back toward the original baseball outfits when the game was played by gentlemen who wore long, white-flannel trousers. The Reds actually reflected the second generation of uniforms, or the first "professional" look. The Reds wore—then and now—highly visible red stockings. Compared with the modish undifferentiated lower uniform, the Reds showed a tiered look with a definite line just below the knee where the grey or white of the trousers met the full red of the sox, and another line where the white undersox met the black shoes.

George Wright, of the original Red Stockings, actually set the standards that Bob Howsam—consciously or not—was following. According to David Voigt, Wright showed a "flair for shrewd showmanship," ordering bright red stockings to complement the white flannel, "a happy choice" that "delighted local fans." Although criticized by some for its garishness, this outfit not only provided the team its nickname, but set a new style for comfortable, tasteful baseball dress ("America's First Red Scare," p. 34).

Was there a hidden advantage in the Reds' style? There is no question that the lower trouser-bottoms make it more difficult to discern the knee line. There is also little question that the modern pitcher has been given a lower strike zone stretching sometimes below the knee, but often excluding anything thrown above the belt. Since these trends are seldom described in the rules of the game, one can do no more than speculate.

The speculation would be that the style of the Reds uniform, showing a clear demarcation below the knee, might earn the batter more "ball" calls on marginal lower pitches; whereas the uniform showing no such demarcation might encourage a more permissive strike call on the borderline low pitches. Furthermore, during the seventies there was said to be a difference in the strike zones between the National and American leagues,

A poster of Woody Woodward in action also illustrates the Reds' traditional look: black shoes, low stirrups, high trousers, a clean shave, and a trim haircut. (Courtesy Cincinnati Reds)

partly because the umpires in one league had abandoned the outside chest protector, allowing them a lower crouch, and thus giving them a better appreciation of the low strike. If this was so, then the Reds' possibly higher strike zone, encouraged by their sartorial style, might have prepared them better for the judgments of umpires from the other league.

Bob Howsam, on reading the above passage, comments that the well-marked kneeline was deliberate and did produce better ball/strike calls. At Denver he had experimented with a complete "strike zone" uniform whose colors matched the ball/strike areas.

The main thrust of the Reds' style was toward making an impression. No one has ever argued that long hair and beards interfere with the game. Yet the Howsam look featured a mandate against facial hair and demanded a neat, short haircut for all actors wearing the Reds costume.

ROBINSON: "The way the Reds looked on the ballfield reminded me of the way the Orioles looked off the field on our road trips. We all wore coats and ties. We all dressed well, and it was a source of team unity and team pride.

"Ballplayers are always testing you. If you give them a little, they'll want more. A guy leaves his tie off one day, the next day he'll show up in jeans just to see if he can get away with it. We stuck by our rules and so did the Reds, and that's good for a team.

"The seventies were a time of social looseness: hippies and all that. Howsam wanted to project the opposite image. To a blue-collar town— even more so when you consider the whole region—Howsam was giving them an old-fashioned, no-nonsense, hardworking look. And they *were* different. That's why I admired Cincinnati."

HOWSAM: "I was working in a market that wanted clean-cut athletes who would have what was considered a good effect on youth. If I were promoting something in Aspen, Colorado, I'd say everyone should have beards and long hair."

PETE: "Yes, the way the Reds looked was all Howsam. I went along with it, but I'm not sure it made sense. I always wondered what would've happened if the whole team showed up one day with shaved heads. He wouldn't've like that, would he? Yet it was not against the rules.

"And suppose this kid had a scarred face resulting from a burn or something. And he wanted to grow a beard to cover the burn marks. Hasn't he a right to do that?

"Maybe I shouldn't say this, but hey, the Big Guy up there has a beard, doesn't He? Lincoln had a beard. George Washington had a beard, eh?"

The *Redsvue* of August 8, 1987 (p. 4), published the following letter under the heading "Setting a Better Example":

To the editor:

The Reds have always had codes against facial hair and, I assume, very long hair. I have always supported these codes because it gives the team a nice, clean look.

However, there is one Red who continues to wear his hair quite long in comparison with his teammates. That is Pete Rose.

Come on, Pete, why don't you set a good example for your players and get a haircut. We surely wouldn't want the Reds to look like Charlie Finley's Oakland A's in the early 1970s.

Scott Pohlkamp
Cincinnati

KLU: "The Reds are still trying to keep that image of the seventies, but Rose is more lenient."

HOWSAM: "A lot of teams are now following the look we created for the Reds, but the Reds themselves are becoming more lax."

STOWE: "Yeah, this year (1987) you'll see three teams going back to more traditional uniforms, including Atlanta, bringing back the old Boston Braves uniform, and Houston, giving up all that yellow shit and wearing a plain white uniform.

"And if you look around the league these days, you'll see only a few beards and mustaches. I'd say less than twenty. Anyway, much less than you used to. The Reds, I think, will always be clean-shaven. Hell, you don't have to say anything to them anymore. In the spring I'd say 80 percent of them come down here to Tampa with beards or mustaches. And they all shave them off. Most of them will tell you the beards are too hot for the Florida weather anyway.

"And you don't see nearly so much long hair anywhere in the big leagues anymore. Yes, I guess you could say the Reds had held on and the other teams are coming around."

PETE: "When they were negotiating with Fingers last spring, they wanted him to agree to shave off his mustache. Hell, they shouldn't ask him to do that! Rollie Fingers's mustache is just as much his trademark as my hustle. They want me to stop hustling? Well, they shouldn't ask him to do away with something that's part of him too.

"Howsam is interested in being unique. If nobody else had the designated hitter, he would want it. As it is we have lost two damn good farm clubs because we couldn't permit them to use the DH."

HOWSAM: "That the distinctive look of the Reds was maintained through the seventies was all due to Sparky Anderson. He gets full credit for that, and it wasn't easy."

Evidently the commitment to the neat, clean-shaven look was congenial to George Anderson, even though he may not have found too many ready disciples. Two different accounts of Sparky's life mention a harsh confrontation with his own son on the issue of personal grooming. Howsam and Anderson both saw the look of the Reds as an antidote to a time when young people seemed to provoke the older generation deliberately with their unkempt appearance. To them this represented not only slovenliness but irresponsibility, and Sparky pictures himself going to the mat with his son on this very issue.

SPARKY: "I honestly think Howsam saved some of the best aspects of baseball tradition by stress on the traditional look. It was the Midwest that saved these traditions, and now they are winning. The rest of the nation is coming back."

BENCH: "On the matter of the way the team looked, I always wondered: if we are supposed to be the leaders, how come nobody—especially the younger people—is following?"

WELSH: "I was a high school pitcher in Cincinnati in the seventies. They invited me down to pitch batting practice; but before they would let me on the field, I had to shave off my mustache. Yes, just for one day of batting practice!"

PEREZ: "The way the Reds look is appropriate to the city. These people expect you to look neat and dress in the traditional way. But that is the way it *should* be!"

CONCEPCION: "Ballplayers, they don't look right with long hair. It looks funny. I don't know about the facial hair, I couldn't grow a beard myself. But maybe a neat mustache looks OK. The way the Reds look fits right in with the city."

Ritter Collett wrote that Anderson willingly enforced the Reds' dress conformity because it "helped people accept the Reds for what they are," then quoted the manager as saying, " 'I honestly believe that part of our appeal to fans in the Cincinnati area is our clean image' " (p. 77). Hal McCoy summarized similarly: "Sparky is convinced that the Cincinnati Reds represent the conservative Midwest. Some of the team's popularity is traced to its clean-cut, well-scrubbed, predictable athletes, he believes," and McCoy finds this "hard to dispute" (p. 24).

Agreed, then, that the appearance of the 1970s Reds was the invention of Bob Howsam, enthusiastically enforced by Sparky Anderson with the cooperation of the team's well-recognized leaders. It was at the least marketing device, at most an expression of certain values. But the Reds' image was more than double-knit deep.

KLU: "Dick Wagner and Sparky had the job of enforcing the Howsam look, but it wouldn't've worked if the star players—Morgan, Rose, Perez, Bench—had not gone along. It worked because of the farm system, where this attitude was taught from the low minors on up. They got rid of the nonconformists before they reached the big leagues."

Were the Reds looking for a certain kind of on-the-field ballplayer? Ted Kluzewski, speaking as a batting coach, complained that they were sending up a bunch of strong-armed jockeys. "Where is the bop!" he lamented. Branch Rickey, one of Bob Howsam's main baseball mentors, preached the gospel according to speed. Speed of foot is the one thing you cannot teach, insisted Mr. Rickey, and Mr. Howsam agreed. But George Weiss, Howsam's other tutor, had a different gospel: balance. You balance speed with power, fastballs with curves, and defensive sureness with offensive daring.

Although the artificial surface put a premium on speed and quickness, it did not dictate a single stereotype. In the end Howsam was influenced as much by Weiss as by Rickey, building a machine of a variety of parts, balanced for the sake of even performance. The athlete, as Howsam and Rose both stress, must perform within his capabilities. If each member of a well-selected team can do that, then the results will exceed the sum of the individual parts. The slugger need not steal bases; the pinch-hitter need not rehearse diving catches in the outfield.

The champion Reds were an aggregation of role-players: Rose for getting on base, Morgan for agitating, Geronimo for covering the green acres, and Tony for knocking them in. There were starters and stoppers; long relievers and specialists at getting left-handed batters to hit ground outs. Most Reds played more than a single role, but they all knew what they were there for and—more important, according to Pete—what they were *not* there for. Joe Morgan, interviewed after the 1976 World Series, spoke for this concept when he declined to characterize the team as having any particular strengths. "We just do," he said, "what it takes to win."

If the Reds' image did not define a particular style of athlete, did it suggest a particular kind of individual? In the view of Ted Kluzewski, the Reds' farm system was a place where nonconformists were weeded out.

HOWSAM: "There are problem players, players who get in a bad rut. But with one or two exceptions we did not deal with problem players. We didn't bring them on the club. I just didn't fool with them.

"I am of the view that a player's attitude off the field is as important as it is on. You hope to find a young man who is happily married and settled, although in today's world that doesn't always work out. But we try to work toward that. Cincinnati is a family city, and we try to be good to the family."

Q: "You are willing to accept less in the way of athletic ability in order to get a young man with the right attitude?"

HOWSAM: "Well, we are hoping to get both. It is our job to scout the whole individual. For example, we didn't have a drug problem on the Cincinnati team because we just wouldn't touch an athlete who was known to have used drugs in high school or in college. We try to know everything about a ballplayer.

"And we try to know even more when we trade for a player. In those cases you don't usually have as much time to learn about the player, so you have to be exceptionally thorough.

"Dave Parker is both an exception and a case in point. He was the first free agent I ever signed, and of course it was public knowledge that he had been involved with drugs. But Dave wanted to come to Cincinnati and had agreed to adopt the kind of image that I said the team must have. And of course it has worked. For the Reds he has been a hard worker and a team leader of the best kind."

Listening to members of the Reds organization and observing baseball in Japan sets up some eerie echoes. The individualistic West is sometimes contrasted with the group-centered East. Even the casual visitor to Japan is struck by the way baseball there reflects some of these cultural differences: the cheering in unison (and near-absence of heckling), the frequent huddles both for strategy and for exhortation, the nearly uniform style of play in all recurring situations. To establish the distinctiveness of baseball Japanese-style, Robert Whiting has resurrected the ancient *bushido*, or Code of the Samurai, and applied it professional baseball in Japan.

ARTICLE: "The player must undergo hard training."

SPARKY: "Bench always called my spring training camp 'Stalag 17.' "

OESTER: "If you want to play for Pete, you better work your butt off."

HOWSAM: "The fans at Riverfront are hardworking people; they expect to see professional, hardworking athletes."

ARTICLE: "The player must demonstrate fighting spirit." Whiting, to illustrate this point, describes the fans' amazement when a batter, after taking a 3–2 pitch, sprinted down the line and slid, headfirst, into the bag. Could it have been a dropped third strike? Well, no, the batter had not even swung. What then? A managerial decree: every batter runs to every base and slides in, headfirst, to demonstrate a "fighting spirit," at least until the corner is turned on a disappointing season.

Would running out a base on balls remind the Cincinnati fan of anyone in particular? How about the trademark of a headfirst slide? And, speaking of fighting spirit, how about a particular headfirst lunge in a special All Star Game?

ARTICLE: "The player must follow the rule of sameness." In the Japanese big leagues, there will be found "no long hair, no goatees, no beards. A player with a handle bar mustache would be accused of 'unsportsmanlike appearance.' " One manager explained that long hair might fit with the artistic or contemplative life, but it did not look good sticking out from under a baseball cap. Nankai Hawk manager Katsuya Nomura, about to take his team on a tour of the United States, ordered short haircuts for all. " 'We don't want the Americans to think we are a bunch of wild men' " (p. 57).

PEREZ: "The people here expect you to look neat . . . but that is the way it *should* be!"

CONCEPCION: "Ballplayers, they don't look right with long hair. It looks funny."

HOWSAM: "If I were promoting skiing in Aspen, I'd say long hair by all means."

ARTICLE: "The player must behave like a good Japanese off the field." If a player is observed in nightclubs, carousing, gambling, or having affairs with unattached women, he will be reprimanded by both the public and management. Getting into public disputes or even traffic violations can cause fines and suspension. The ideal player, asked to state his life's dream, replies, " 'I want to get married and live together with my mother and my wife.' "

KLU: "They get rid of the nonconformists in the farm system."

HOWSAM: "You hope to find a young man who is happily married and settled . . . we just wouldn't touch an athlete who was known to have used drugs. . . ."

To test these parallels further requires substituting something for "a good Japanese"; but what? Certainly not "a good American"; the United States contains too many different cultures to be compared with relatively homogeneous Japan. "Behave like a good Cincinnatian?" This is just funny; the response would be: "Is there such a thing as a good Cincinnatian?" and so forth. To say that the Reds wanted ballplayers that fit in with the midwestern lifestyle is much better, perhaps as close as one gets to answering the complex question that keeps plaguing this chapter.

The Reds attempted to project a distinctive image, on the field and—to some extent—off the field as well. This attitude was also reflected in the way Riverfront Stadium was sited, serviced, and maintained. At what audience was this image directed?

That there is more than one answer to this question is what makes the Reds of the 1970s fascinating, both as a baseball team and as a window into the culture. The broad-scale answer to this question emerges slowly as one listens to Sparky Anderson, David Concepcion, Bob Howsam, Tony Perez, Brooks Robinson, Bernie Stowe, and—perhaps especially—Pete Rose. No one of these people comes right out and says that the Reds were history's team, but they come very close to it.

Baseball has all kinds of elements in its past, clean and dirty, savory and smelly, heroic and corrupt. But most Americans think of baseball as the national game. They like to think of it as a sport where the individual and the team combine to stage contests where hard work and ability triumph over chance and subversion. Its heroes should have those qualities that can properly influence the young; the total game should be acceptable to the total society.

When Sparky Anderson says that the greatest thing Bob Howsam did was to preserve the best traditions of the game, he is not just talking about a clean shave. When Bob Howsam talks about the way the Reds put Cincinnati on the map, he is not just talking about a winning decade; he is talking about a style that meets particular standards. To Atanasio Rigal Perez and David Ismael Concepcion, coming from a slightly different American culture, there was something that seemed right about the Reds of the 1970s; this was professional baseball as it ought to be. When Pete Rose tells people, as he always does, that Cincinnati is the "baseball capital of the world," he points to innovation and leadership; he clearly suggests that the Reds are the keepers of baseball's best traditions.

Ritter Collett, describing the confrontation of Cincinnati and New York in the World Series of 1976, gives a particular stress to this notion. Coming as it did on the eve of baseball's new era of free agentry, accelerated hype, and million-dollar, multiyear contracts, this matchup seemed to pit the unsentimental future against the recognizable past. Markets such as New York City would surely come to dominate a world where baseball talent was directly up for sale as it had dominated the nation's media networks. Against this looming future where talent would be crassly auctioned, the Reds represented "an old-fashioned team concept" blending the individual talents of well-paid athletes. Baseball people throughout the nation, thought Collett, "were rooting for the Reds against the Yankees because they represented baseball's traditional image so well": an image under imminent attack (p. 13).

Collett's selection of the Yankees as the counterfoil to the Reds was apt indeed; for the Cincinnati style defined itself most clearly by what it was *not*. It was definitely not New York. Sparky Anderson becomes emotional when describing the crowd behavior at Shea Stadium following the conclusion of the playoff against the Mets in 1973. "These people were animals. They spit on our people, tore at their clothes. We had a United States senator in our party, and we had to take him out through the clubhouse after the crowd had cleared."

For Bob Howsam, the great triumph of his team was marred by the threat of Yankee Stadium violence in '76. "We had to send security people there ahead of time. They advised us to sit in the rear of the stadium and wear dark clothes. We couldn't even cheer our own team without running the risk of abuse."

For Ted Kluzewski, New York has two strikes. One is the threat of violence. In the summer of 1986 he recounted his last visit to the Apple. He had eaten at his favorite Manhattan restaurant, then asked the owner to call him a cab. "They won't stop here anymore after dark," he was told. So Klu had to walk the five blocks to his midtown hotel. "I was scared every inch of the way. I walked at the edge of the sidewalk, as far away from the building fronts as I could get. I kept looking over my shoulder. I wouldn't want to do that again." For the rest of us who had always thought that a physique like his would render us totally fearless, the idea of a petrified Klu is almost too much. Strike one.

KLU: "When Roy McMillan went to the Mets in 1964, he was thirty-four years old. Suddenly a star was born. They saw the way he played his position, which was something to see. But Mac was already just a little bit past it. It was as though those ten years of sensationial play in Cincinnati had never happened. If it doesn't happen in New York it doesn't count." Strike two.

The Cincinnati style is clearly an alternative to that of the Big Apple. It is also explicitly opposed to the other coast. The Reds' look is defined by many of the players as the opposite to Charlie Finley's Oakland team with its subsidized handlebars and its three-color, mix-and-match double-knits, reminding various of the Reds of clowns or Sunday softball teams. The Reds also see themselves as projecting an opposite image to the

The Reds and their fans demonstrate a regional character in both negative and positive ways. TOP: Cincinnati fans mock New York hype by questioning the celebrity of great Yankee catcher Thurman Munson. (Courtesy *Cincinnati Enquirer*) RIGHT: Pitcher Tom Browning, showing he knows where milk comes from, takes part in Farmers Night, an annual event at Riverfront. (Courtesy Cincinnati Reds)

hippie drug culture, whose headquarters during this era was in the Haight-Ashbury district of San Francisco, that libertine metropolis across the bay.

ROBINSON: "Cincinnati is a blue-collar, workingman's town, and the surrounding region is the same, only more so. The only place this style would take hold is in the Midwest: Kansas City; St. Louis maybe." Brooks Robinson, who likes the Reds' style, grew up in Arkansas, it should be noted, and picked as similar the two big-league cities closest to his old home.

SPARKY: "The Reds were deliberately offered to a regional market. They did studies of this. More tickets were sold outside the city than inside. At one time I think 20 percent of the tickets were sold in Dayton."

HOWSAM: "Cincinnati is ideally located. It is a hundred miles from Columbus, a hundred miles from Indianapolis, a hundred miles from Louisville and from Lexington. The Reds play to a whole region."

BENCH: "Cincinnati fans come from Tennessee, West Virginia, northern Ohio, and Kentucky. The area is like that surrounding St. Louis and Kansas City, but it is also different. Fans here stay to the end of the game because they know what is going on. Also there is no rush. Most people are here for a whole series, and they're not going anywhere they can't walk."

PARKER: "The Reds have a great drawing area: northern Ohio, Indiana, West Virginia, Kentucky. The city itself is one of the smaller ones in the big leagues, but that does not mean they have a small budget. They can keep this park full. All they have to do is win."

Hal McCoy, in defending the distinctiveness of the Cincinnati image, argues: "Where else could a baseball franchise offer a Farm Night and have 40,000 fans show up, all hopeful of winning a tractor, a pickup truck or a cow in a post-game drawing?" (p. 24)

KLU: "People sometimes think of this as an area of straitlaced farmers, but that's not fair. They are down-the-middle. They are beautiful people."

Ray Knight, wearing the uniform of the New York Mets when interviewed, said: "Of course baseball draws well here. What else is there to do?" Objectively, there is some truth in this remark, even though it will provoke automatic resentment from the proud residents of the Queen City. The problem with Knight's judgment is that it fails totally to understand how Cincinnati is viewed by the fans who come from outside the city: the ones whose tendencies were closely studied by Mayor Ruehlmann and his colleagues.

In this respect Cincinnati is no different from the other midwestern cities that exist in the center of a hinterland. The local metropolis may not be Paris, but it is close enough. Uncle John, who sells cars outside Portsmouth, puts the family in the pickup or gets up a party of three couples and takes the Buick four-door. They get their box seats well in advance and book rooms at the newest downtown hotel. In the morning there will be a fancy brunch at the hotel. The women will raid the department stores and boutiques; the men surround a couple of cold ones while watching the parade of local talent. There may even be some real business done at a bank or a regional marketing headquarters.

If it does not interfere with the game, there will be a motion to attend a concert or play. With family history as a growing pastime, some member of the party may consult the records of an archive or historical society. If the group is in luck, they may be part of one of Danny Ransohoff's famous tours of the city. In former times there might have been a visit to a northern Kentucky casino; now there will at least be one memorable meal at one of the city's many inviting restaurants.

The trip will last two or three days. Brought home will be a couple of well-thumbed scorecards, but also a new dress and sportshirt. Souvenirs may include a Reds pennant, more likely a number of charge-card flimsies from bars and restaurants. If the team has won, this is fine; but it is not really essential. What has happened here is what used to be called "steppin' out" and is now called "glitz." The ball team has furnished an excuse—preferably a victorious excuse—for the classic function of the city toward its hinterland.

Gordy Coleman, who directs the Reds Speakers Bureau and doubtless knows the team's market first-hand, reinforces the notion that the Reds are "our team" in parts of a five-state area. He cites "the Rosey Reds" as the largest organization of female fans attached to any big-league team. They not only attend Riverfront en masse, but organize trips to spring training and to regular-season road games. Gordy thinks that special promotions and regional habits combine to make this team unparalleled in their appeal to women and to family groups.

Who actually buys tickets to see the Reds at Riverfront? This is not easy to discover, and even if one knew, he would also know that the ticket is only part of the story. In 1986, according to Janet Wendel, director of season sales, only 28 percent of the season tickets were sold outside "the Greater Cincinnati area," a term often used to include parts of three states. And who knows whether Uncle John bought his tickets by mail in Portsmouth or at the downtown Reds office in Cincinnati? What is safe to say is that the Reds, under Bob Howsam, developed an image that was seen as having several facets.

To the nation at large, the Reds tried to represent the best elements in the "old-fashioned" approach to the game. In contrast to the coastal cultures, the Reds made a sartorial, tonsorial, and deportmental statement against the big-city Babylons on the coasts and in favor of the heartland. They were clean-cut, hard-working, talented athletes offering a team performance suitable for the whole family. The values were those associated with the Midwest, but not with all of the Midwest.

ROBINSON: "Cincinnati is not Detroit. That is a sort of tougher, one-industry, union town."

BELL: "What is the difference between Cleveland and Cincinnati? A whole world."

WELSH: "What irks me about Florida is how they lump all Ohioans together. They see all those green-and-white license plates and think we are all part of one great migration. They don't begin to realize how distinctive Cincinnati is, compared with the rest of the state."

PARKER: "I have lived and worked in two so-called blue-collar, working-class cities, and they are nothing alike. In Pittsburgh everybody works hard and hates it; in Cincinati they all work hard and love it."

In order to fine-tune the regional appeal of the Reds, one should probably think again about the city's railroad, about the broadcast networks, and about the wisdom of Arkansan Brooks Robinson. The Reds' image is accepted at just that place where the Midwest meets the South: right down the westward extension of Mason and Dixon's line. Reds country is Mid-America, further defined by what we learned, in the nineteenth century, to call the border states: the northernmost part of the South and the southernmost part of the North, but all in the valley of the Ohio.

As to whether the image of the Reds was designed with the city or the region in mind, Bob Howsam should have the last word: "The way we presented the Reds was very pleasing to the people of the region and to the people who lived in the city."

The point of quoting a few articles from Robert Whiting's book on Japanese professional baseball (chap. 3) is not to suggest that the Reds of the seventies were the Toyotas of the National League. Of the twelve principles in the baseball *bushido*, more than half would be laughable if applied to the Reds or to any other American team. That is part of Whiting's point. Although the Japanese borrowed baseball from the United States, they don't play it the same way. The sport and its context can be used to understand Japanese culture: especially in contrast with that of the United States.

Understanding baseball is a key to understanding Japan, asserts Whiting persuasively. Baseball helps explain America; furthermore, different teams can sometimes help in understanding regional and cultural difference within the heterogeneous United States. In the 1970s, at least, no American team worked harder to represent one part of the country than did the Reds to represent midwestern traditions and values.

In a *few* ways the Reds can be understood as resembling the Japanese in their attitude more than they resemble some of their American competition. These are the ways that center on hard work, dedication to maximum effort, and off-field deportment aligned with community expectations. The Reds, a group of well-defined individuals, went a way toward showing that—even in a highly individualistic sport—a bunch of individuals can give the appearance of conformity and project the image of a region.

The puzzle of American life is the blending of individualism with democracy, personal liberty with concern for the community. One reason why baseball is a fitting representation of the national personality is that it, too, demands a subtle blend of the unique person and the collective effort. The Reds of the 1970s created this balance before a large national audience and did so in a manner that was unprecedentedly keyed to a distinct regional audience.

Chapter Four.....
THE NEEDLE
AND THE SPARK

Buddy Bell, returning to his locker from the buffet in the players' lounge: "Hey, Bernie. Nice melon."

Bernie Stowe, a fixture in the clubhouse since the days of Buddy's father, appears in the equipment manager's doorway: "Thanks, Buddy."

BELL: "It's about time."

STOWE: "You sleazy backbiting mackerel-grabbing sonofabitch, you wouldn't know good fruit from monkey shit. Last time you even thought you knew what you were doing was before Texas smartened up and got rid of your lazy ass. . . . "

The tirade continues—more pungent and detailed than can be reproduced. It is a small masterpiece of scatology and applied invective. With each phrase Bell's grin approaches his ears as finally Stowe, unable to maintain the feigned anger, pops back into his chamber for a nostalgic chuckle. Here, in this 1986 exchange, is an echo of the banter that made the Reds of the 1970s almost as famous for their needling as they were for their victories.

All good teams have their stars and their strong personalities. All must find a way to burnish individual excellence with the buffers of group pressure. The failure to learn this trick—never an easy one—often robs a team of its best performance. The potential for disunity rises in proportion to the number of exceptional performers. The Reds of the 1970s certainly had more than their share.

Ritter Collett, who followed the Reds on a daily basis and wrote *Men of the Reds Machine*, saw fit to draw fifteen separate portraits before dealing with such collectives as "the staff," "the bullpen," and those "who also served." Six of these were pitchers:: Gary Nolan, Don Gullett, Fred Norman, Rawley Eastwick, Jack Billingham, and Pat Zachry. Although, as Bob Howsam says, somebody must have been throwing the ball pretty well for a team to win 210 regular plus 14 postseason games in two consecutive years, the baseball public has not been quick to place the mound staff on the same plateau with the rest of the team. This may not be fair in light of Gullett's power when at his prime or Billingham's series record; but it is likely to stick. No one in 1975 and '76 won more than fifteen games; and no starter, save Gullett in 1975, had an earned-run average under three. For the sake of appreciating the sparkle of the roster, it is not necessary to belabor the point: there was enough luster among the starting eight.

As of September, 1987, three of the 1970s Reds are still active. Dan Driessen sparked the division-leading Cardinals over the Cubs, collecting three singles and driving in a vital run in a 5–3 victory. Ken Griffey is putting in a creditable year in the Atlanta outfield and, with less than three weeks left in the season, is batting .284 with fourteen homers and sixty-three runs batted in for a team near the bottom of its division. David Concepcion, showing few signs of age, has played five positions for the 1987 Reds and in 234 at bats was hitting .291, including three game-winning runs batted in, through August 31. Clearly, it is too early to pronounce a final judgment on some of the players, but it is not too early to be impressed.

Ken Griffey, born in 1950, learned his baseball on the hard gravel of a housing development in the mill town of Donora, Pennsylvania, already placed firmly on the baseball map by native son Stan Musial. In high school, seeing a college scholarship as the way up, he played football but never really liked it. Still a skinny lad of eighteen and scarcely tutored in the art of the diamond, he brought two ingredients essential in the Rickey/Howsam recipe: speed and a settled family life. With these assets he survived a slow start and an unfamiliar environment.

Fortunately for all concerned, Griffey ran into some of the more patient members of the Reds system: particularly Russ Nixon, his minor-league manager, and Brooks Lawrence, a former pitcher who had traveled the South in the days of legal segregation. Steadily, Ken learned to solve some problems and cope with others. His family flourished as his physique matured to a muscular 190 pounds on a 5'11" frame. The increased strength cost him no speed. He was clocked to first in 3.5 seconds. Thirty-eight infield hits helped lift his average over .300 in his first full Cincinnati year, and his thirty-four well-placed stolen bases were part of the '76 Redleg magic.

Of all the Reds of the 1970s who tend to be overlooked, George Kenneth Griffey may deserve neglect the least. He covered right field more than adequately and, along with Pete Rose, specialized in getting on base where Bench, Doggie, and the rest could bring him home. His batting average was almost enough to win the crown in '76; only a perfect final day by Bill Madlock deprived Ken of the top spot. Consistency has been his forte, however, as attested by a composite average, after twelve years, of .302, better than any of his teammates save only Rose. His bat, his batting eye, his exceptional speed of foot, and his sound baserunning judgment combined to allow him to score a prodigious 413 runs during his and the Reds' four prime years. Although not near the center of the clubhouse three-ring circus, Griffey has been popular with his mates, a cheerful man with a ready and contagious laugh. He married early and has remained a settled family man. Productive, quiet, good-natured, Ken Griffey fit the Cincinnati style, and he promptly made that city his home. (Material in this section from Collett, McCoy, Rathgeber.)

Dan Driessen, still active as is Griffey, is parallel in other ways. Dan was born just a year later than Ken and grew up in a black, working-class environment. Like Griffey he had speed and a willingness to work; also he had such a quick, fierce, natural swing that Sparky christened him the Cobra. Reds management thought so highly of this hitting potential that they eventually made their biggest mistake of the 1970s: trading Tony Perez. To be sure, they tried the Cobra at third base and in the outfield. At his original position, catching, he showed no true aptitude. Only first base was left. The eight-year age difference between the two first basemen was also a factor; and the Reds, according to both Howsam and Anderson, never realized the intangible value of Perez until he was gone.

About the same size as Griffey, Driessen is always spoken of as fast "for a big man." He did in fact steal fifty-nine bases in 1977 and '78 combined. In his first twelve years, all but fifty-one games with the Reds, Dan Driessen, a seemingly relaxed, perpetually smiling 187-pounder, hit 142 home runs, knocked in 702, and scored 682: not bad for a man who was really a utility player for his first four years.

If there were a prize for being inconspicuous, it would go, without debate, to a handsome six-foot centerfielder with a warm, dimpled smile, who always looked tall because of his long legs and slim, 165-pound physique. Cesar Francisco Geronimo was born in El Seybo, Dominican Republic, in 1948. That he would end up an outfielder for Cincinnati was a most unlikely projection of a career that began with enrollment in a Jesuit seminary.

When Cesar discovered in baseball a rival for his religious inclinations, it was the Spanish-language broadcasts of Yankee games that made him a disciple of the Pinstripers, the organization that first signed him. Bringing to hardball an uppercutting slow-pitch softball swing, he hit so poorly in the low minors that he was surprised not to be tried as a pitcher or released outright. Having moved to Houston, Geronimo began to make his mark as an exceptional centerfielder, even though his hitting was still far from strong. Sparky Anderson, by his own admission, repeatedly urged his boss to conclude a deal for Morgan rather than jeopardize it by keeping after "the Chief."

Howsam persisted, Cesar became part of "the Trade," and batting instructor Kluzewski was presented with the "worst batting stroke" he had ever seen on a major-leaguer. Geronimo's throwing arm and defensive skills were already approaching legendary status. Howsam was thinking of the expansive Riverfront outfield and of the fact that no effective replacement for Bobby Tolan had been found. "But did you really think Geronimo would learn to hit?" I asked Howsam. "Well, we weren't sure he would hit; but we were sure of this: he had never been given a real chance to show whether he could or couldn't."

Geronimo will never be remembered as a slugger, but he surely did improve. Klu's tutelage helped eliminate the uppercutting. Sparky's prescription of occasional off days and a respite from winter ball did much to preserve the strength of this relatively fragile player. His batting average rose sporadically but steadily to an impressive .310 in 1976. He stole twenty-two bases that same year, and his manager called him "the best number eight hitter in baseball."

Less debatable were the Chief's defensive skills. His colleagues resented the fact that his counterparts playing in New York City tended to get more attention, but his five consecutive Gold Gloves speak for the recognition of his peers. Quiet in the extreme, a religiously inclined man in the most profane of settings, Cesar Geronimo was the best defensive centerfielder of his decade.

One year younger than Cesar, George Foster shared his religious inclination, reading the Bible and religious commentaries, loving to discourse on reincarnation, and tending toward shyness. In other ways, Foster, the Chief's ultimate neighbor in the outfield, was his opposite. If Cesar was a bit fragile, Foster gave new meaning to "robust." More than an inch taller than Cesar, George never seemed so because of his massive shoulders and arms. Slim of waist and hip, Foster played at 180 pounds but looked twice as wide in the upper torso. Whereas Cesar was silent, George spoke in a high, squeaky voice that contrasted comically with his physique.

Fans cherish a mental kinescope of George streaking across the foul line, snaring a twisting drive, then pivoting those broad shoulders to snap off a throw to the plate, doubling an overconfident runner. There were also times when Foster seemed unconcerned in the field, in marked contrast to his neighbor who was forever chasing baseballs into fences and digging them out of the turf. At bat Cesar hit, at best, soft liners and grounders through the infield. Foster, on the other hand, *always* hit the ball hard. He is one of only eight men to hit over 50 home runs in a single season, and his career total, after sixteen years in the majors, was 313, many of them spectacular. On August 3, 1977, he propelled a ball along a trajectory which, had it not hit the stands, would have landed 720 feet from where it was struck, according to the best estimates of the "flight" engineers.

George was a vital part of the Big Red Machine. It is conceded that Pete Rose's shift to third, allowing George to play left field regularly, was the key to two successive World Championships. In 1976 George led the league with 121 RBIs, yet was always being overshadowed or suffering from poor timing. Against the Yankees in the '76 Series, for example, George hit .429 and batted in four runs in four games. As his luck would seem to have it, however, Johnny Bench hit .522, including four home runs, played a set of beautiful defensive games, and easily earned the MVP award.

The next year George Foster led everybody but Dolly Parton: 52 homers, 124 runs, 149 runs batted in, with a batting average of .320 and an incredible slugging percentage of .631 (better than all but one of Stan Musial's seasons). This won him the season's MVP award—that record could hardly have been ignored—but instead of leading his team through another World Series, George saw the Reds finish ten games behind the despised Dodgers, a sickening comedown for the spoiled Queen City fans.

After 1977 Foster's performance declined steadily though not precipitously. He played out his Reds contract, became a free agent after 1981, and joined the Mets with a large, multiyear contract, only to fall so short of his halcyon days as to evoke the charge of lessened effort. A man of intelligence, discipline, and enormous strength, Foster left gargantuan records and, even so, failed to meet his potential. Devoted to his mother, who had moved from Alabama to raise her son in California, George sometimes seemed torn by other influences. Pleasant, sober, abstemious, sometimes humorous, he was also at times withdrawn. Collett calls him "the Different One."

A row of lockers assigned to Griffey, Driessen, Geronimo, and Foster might be as quiet as a church pew. Based on a first impression, the soft-spoken, ingratiating shortstop from Aragua, Venezuela, might seem to promise no great disruptive potential; this impression would be mistaken.

"Tell me about the time Concepcion was spinning around in the clubhouse clothes dryer," I asked Connie Barthelmas of the Reds publicity

Lined up before the opening game of the 1976 World Series are, *left to right*, Dave Concepcion, Cesar Geronimo, Johnny Bench, George Foster, Dan Driessen, Tony Perez, Joe Morgan, Ken Griffey, and Pete Rose. (Courtesy *Cincinnati Enquirer*)

office. "I don't know any details," she replied, "but if there was any kind of shenanigans going on down there, I would bet a lot of money that Davey started it!"

This kind of reputation, apparently deserved, contrasts sharply with the picture of a skinny, nervous youngster signed by the Cincinnati organization at the age of nineteen. Although his strong arm had gained him some local celebrity as a pitcher, Davey had seen his graceful countryman, Luis Aparicio, play the winter season and had determined to follow in those agile footsteps. The way was not easy. The Reds had plenty of promising shortstops, even including another Venezuelan, Virgilio Mata, who looked like better all-around athletes than the gangling kid of 6'2" who didn't reach his mature playing weight of 155 pounds until many years later. Class A pitching seemed to intimidate him. His meager English, strongly accented, made life in America difficult, as did the attitude in some of the small southern towns toward anyone of his complexion.

But Concepcion also had a lot going for him. He had abundant speed and ran the bases with skill and abandon. His large frame added to the range his quickness provided, and his "cannon" enabled him to nail a baserunner even from deep in the hole. Although he was built like a scarecrow, he became a miracle of coordinated fluidity once he slipped on the fielder's glove and crouched, in anticipation, between second and third. Anderson was among the discerning baseball judges who realized very quickly that they were looking at a truly exceptional shortstop.

Ted Kluzewski, returning to the Reds as hitting instructor just as Davey was entering the system, reportedly liked the young man's swing from the start and was surprised to see how much strength resided in the thin wrists and arms. And, in spite of a dubious beginning as a batter, Davey learned to handle the best of big-league pitching, steadily improving his plate performance until he thrice topped .300 (1978, 1981, 1987). Even more important, he became a clutch hitter, batting an even .300 in postseason play with twelve World Series runs batted in. Friends and foes alike began to realize that, even on a team of sluggers, Davey was a most dangerous man at the plate in a close game with runners on base. He did in fact lead his illustrious teammates of the 1970s in the number of game-winning RBIs.

For a man whose father had wanted him to be a doctor, Davey remains squeamish at the sight of blood; for a willing prankster, he can still be unsettled by a bad review of his sartorial statements. But the answer to his general moodiness was provided by Sparky Anderson, who seemed to regard the youngster as a second son, and who made team leader Tony

Perez Davey's designated big brother. "All the big stars of the Reds instinctively knew how to get along with people, including the press," said Sparky. "That is, they all did except Davey, and Doggie taught him how to do it."

No one had to teach Davey how to play shortstop, and no one overestimated his ability. Chosen regularly for the All Star teams, and awarded five successive Gold Gloves, Concepcion is, in the judgment of many, the premier defensive shortstop of the 1970s, as well as a hitter who more than holds his own. Davey wanted to be as celebrated in Venezuela as was Aparicio when he himself was young. He had his wish. There will be many surprised baseball fans in both Americas if the name David Ismael Bonitez Concepcion is not one day writ large in Cooperstown.

When Johnny Bench was just twenty-two years old, his team was playing a spring exhibition against the Washington Senators, then managed by Ted Williams. Johnny asked Ted for his autograph and was astounded to read "To Johnny, a Hall of Famer for sure." The Splendid Splinter, never generous with his praise, had recognized what a lot of people suspected. The part-Indian native of Binger, Oklahoma, with the broad shoulders and huge hands, would be seriously considered by many as the best at his position the game had ever seen.

Bench got there in a hurry. After batting only once for the Tampa farm team, he was installed as the starter, and the team's other catcher was dismissed. The Cincinnati manager, when Bench was still in the minors, advised the management that their present catcher could be traded. In his third full major-league season Johnny hit forty-five homers, batted in 148 runs, and became the youngest person ever to win the Most Valuable Player award. Two years later he won it again.

Like Ted Williams, Bench also had a knack for the dramatic, from hitting a game-tying homer in the last game played at Crosley Field, to capping the team's unmatched postseason surge of '76 with a fantastic World Series performance climaxed by two crushing Yankee Stadium home runs in the finale. His home run off Dave Giusti in the ninth inning rescued the '72 playoffs at the very last moment and was labeled at that time as the most important hit in the Reds' history.

Overcoming the original shyness of a small-town kid away from home, Bench became a public figure. He sang country-and-western songs with famous performers; he visited the White House at the request of President Ford; he played in celebrity golf tournaments and headed charity drives. The nation's fans made him the leading All Star vote-getter from 1973 to 1975. At his wedding to Vicki Chesser in 1975, police cordons restrained the crowds from a ceremony to which the president of the U.S. and a glittering array of celebrities had been invited.

Yet success and popularity never brought to Bench the easy disposition that he might have envied. At times convivial, usually articulate, Bench can also be a loner. Plagued by a series of accidents, injuries, and health scares, the big catcher confesses the cynicism of one who rose early to the top and thence often failed to measure up to the expectations of others. Johnny had a touching fourteen-month friendship with a moribund leukemia victim from nearby Dayton who eventually died at the age of five. Commenting on the marvel of this relationship, the lad's mother confessed that Johnny often seemed more the boy, and her son the adult. Chided for his social-climbing wedding invitations, Bench responded that he knew all his intended guests and that all the celebrities had replied to their invitations, even though most of them did not attend. A year after this festive bonding, Vicki was calling her husband "a true tragedy as a person" (Collett, pp. 149–50).

The celebrity of Johnny Lee Bench, born in Binger, Oklahoma, on December 7, 1947, makes it difficult to throw any new light upon him. His seventeen years in the majors, all with the Reds, mark him as at least one of the best men ever to play his position: as a handler of pitchers, as a fielder, as a menace to thieving baserunners, and as a power hitter par excellence. In the clubhouse he was a top celebrity: at times a needler and a catalyst, at times a man still trying to ponder his own private meanings.

When you accept the role of celebrity, you make your inner life your outer life. You have to accept the fact that your estranged wife will say unkind things about you in public and that the public will be interested. Paternity suits and divorces will make the newspapers. Neither Johnny Bench nor Pete Rose has shied away from celebrity—from making commercial endorsements to skillfully entertaining the press. The reader needs little help in imagining either of them in a clubhouse situation, even though their roles would be quite different.

Bench cherished the poker games at the back of the plane, but reserved the right to go off by himself. Rose was the appointed busybody. He could come up to any player, face off with him eyeball to eyeball, staring him down with his half-petitioning, half-challenging expression, and offer him anything from a bucking up to a dressing down, or just the latest vile joke. He was Captain Pete, by word of Sparky, and by acclaim.

Bench and Rose were more familiar to the public than the other Reds, but the clubhouse leaders were—in everyone's estimation—Tony Perez,

Joe Morgan, and Captain Pete. This triumvirate ruled for a number of reasons, the most obvious being that they spoke for the three prominent racial/ethnic groups that roughly divided the roster and which often exactly divided the starting lineup. On a typical game day in the mid-1970s the Reds would field three Latin Americans (Geronimo, Perez, Concepcion), three black Americans (Morgan, Griffey, Foster), and three Americans of European ancestry, one with a fraction of Indian blood (Bench, Rose, and the starting pitcher). In the locker room, where race is seldom a forbidden subject, the Cincinnati clubhouse recognized this demarcation and appointed, in effect, a leader for each division.

Pete Rose was the first and, in most ways, the most natural team leader to emerge. Born in 1941, he is the oldest of the three, although not by much (Perez is a year younger; Morgan, two). He was supremely at home: not just because leadership came naturally but also because he *was* at home, playing the game he loves best in his home town, the city he loves best.

Age and confidence would have meant little if Pete had not also led by example. Famous for running out bases on balls and turning singles into doubles, Pete was an overachiever in ways that even his admiring public might not fully appreciate. Kluzewski marvels that, whereas most hitters begin to tighten up or start blistering after ten minutes in the batting cage, Rose could go on hitting, pitch after pitch, for up to thirty or even forty minutes. Nor did he ever seem to lose his concentration. Again according to Klu, Rose could be shown any segment of game film made while he was batting and, from watching a single pitch, run the whole game forward or backward from memory. "Oh yeah. That was Carlton trying his curve on a two-and-two count; sixth inning; one out, two on. He had got me to ground into a double play on that same effing curve in the third. And the Chief had singled off his fastball before Freddy lucked out on the overthrow. So I was looking for the curve, only not in that spot. Next time he started me with it. . . . "

For reasons baseball fans do not really need to be told, the magnetic, unavoidable, indefatigable Pete Rose occupied one of three senior chairs in the clubhouse. Although it is hard to imagine things happening otherwise, it was a great day for the Reds when the new manager made the hometown hero the team captain, and when the captain returned the confidence by offering to do anything he could to make the manager's plans work among the players.

Another great nonplaying decision—comparable to having Concepcion room with Perez on the road—was having Bernie Stowe put Joe Morgan's locker next to that of Captain Pete, thus making allies of two strong personalities that might easily have become antagonistic. Joseph Leonard Morgan, born in Bonham, Texas, grew up in Oakland. Standing 5'7", Morgan always detested references to his size and signed with the Astros because theirs was the only scout who made no reference to his being "a good *little* ballplayer." Unlike the many Reds who came from small towns, Joe grew up "street smart," like his neighbor Pete, and quickly fell in with the sharp banter that filled the pregame air.

Morgan has what the players call a "motormouth." Furthermore, he came to Cincinnati with a reputation for friction with the management: in particular with Houston manager Harry Walker. But he proved two things very quickly. One was that he could thrive in an environment where he was but one star among many, as opposed to having been a relatively lonely celebrity with the Astros. The Reds players showed him something, he later acknowledged, about discipline and teamwork.

Morgan also proved that, motormouth or not, he had some important things to say. He brought with him, for example, a "book" on every Reds pitcher, which not only helped him steal bases but also showed patterns and keys valuable to hitters. The skeptical pitching coach Larry Shepard admitted that Joe had done his homework well. Throughout his career with the Reds, he accepted the role of unpaid stealing coach, most notably as the force behind "Morgan's Raiders," whose disturbingly aggressive tactics turned the tide against the Pirates and Red Sox in the 1975 postseason series. Sparky says he would make a great manager, except that he always has so much going on. Pete calls him the smartest baseball man he has ever known.

As the second of the three group leaders, Morgan earned his place by more than brains and volubility. His particular fetish was to work on *all* aspects of the game; to become the game's best all-around player. Speed and quickness gave him natural advantages both at the plate and in the field. Study improved his baserunning just as continuing work with Ted Kluzewski sharpened his timing and repressed his bad habits. If there was a chink in Morgan's all-around prowess, it was his throwing arm, adequate for his position but not outstanding. Throughout his career, he kept working at stretching and strengthening exercises designed to remove this one flaw.

As an offensive weapon, it is hard to conceive of anyone more totally effective than "Mighty Joe." His best years were also the team's best years. In 1975 Joe batted .327, stole 67 bases, and scored 107 runs while knocking in 94. The next year he hit .320, stole 60 bases, struck 27 home runs, batted in 111, and scored 113 runs. His slugging average—a composite of consistency and power—led the league (.576). Playing alongside

Practical joker Concepcion makes sure that Doggie Perez, king of the put-down, gets a share of effervescence. (Courtesy Cincinnati Reds)

the breaker of Ty Cobb records and the best catcher of his era, Morgan nonetheless won two consecutive MVP awards: 1975 and 1976.

HOWSAM: "Joe Morgan is the best all-around offensive ballplayer I have ever seen."

SPARKY: "When all is said and done, Morgan's the best thing Howsam ever done. He is so talented it is unbelievable. He changed the destiny of the team."

PEREZ: "Joe's the complete player. Especially he was in '75 and '76. There were times when he carried the whole team. No one could be more valuable."

Here they are, the team's daily starters in the mid-1970s: their value on the playing field; personalities. The roster, presented in no categorical order, nonetheless reaches a kind of climax in Joe Morgan, whom Ritter Collett calls "the ultimate." Yet has not everyone testified that Johnny Lee Bench is the ultimate catcher? And who is the standard against whom all future hitters and hustlers will be measured if not the Ty Cobb of the 1970s, Pete Rose? Yet as great as were these three—and several among their teammates—not one of them was ever called "top dog."

"Doggie" was born Atanasio Rigal Perez in Camaguey, Cuba, on May 14, 1942. When scout Tony Pacheco brought the skinny kid to a tryout camp, he was already deceptively strong from lifting the heavy sugar sacks in the mill whose constant noise he loathed. Pacheco, to whom Perez remains demonstrably grateful, corrected his grip on the bat to make him a pull hitter, and persuaded him to learn several defensive positions in anticipation of the unpredictable future.

One thing everyone noticed about young Tony in Tampa, in the spring of 1967, was his even disposition. Good days and bad, he showed his lovely smile. Competitive but not jealous, the young Cuban bore no apparent grudges. Given the chance, he would treat everyone like family. "Just don't send me back to the sugar mill."

Over the years these characteristics were enhanced in certain ways. As the political situation in Cuba hardened under Castro, Tony had to give up seeing his own family or risk being confined to the island. Instead he began wintering in Puerto Rico, where he met and married Juana de la Cantera, known to her mainland friends as Pituka. With a disposition as pleasant and outgoing as that of her husband, Pituka has been loved wherever she has gone, becoming a kind of big sister to the wives of the young players, a legend of helpfulness to those who have had problems in adapting to a new environment. Tony, carrying with him a cargo of warmth for the family he could no longer see in Cuba, invested it in his wife and two sons, making the Perez family a model of mutual love and support.

Young Tony also made some particular baseball friendships that were to be as important as they were lasting. When he was assigned to the Geneva, New York, farm club in '67, who should be playing Tony's favored spot but a perky kid from Cincinnati just one year older than he. Tony switched to third base so that Pete Rose could continue at second, and an enduring friendship began. From 1964 to 1976, Rose and Perez were teammates on the Reds. After Pete moved to Philadelphia, Tony joined him there in time for the 1983 pennant. When Pete came back to Cincinnati in 1984, Perez quickly followed, occasionally replacing the "older" Rose on first and contributing eleven pinch hits. Retiring as a player, Tony became a member of the Reds coaching staff in 1987. Pete and Tony share a capacity for friendship and loyalty. A large part of the force that moved the Reds through their best years was built on a cornerstone of this particular alliance: Pete and Tony.

The most obvious value of the strong Cuban was his ability to knock in runs. For ten consecutive years with Cincinnati (and another with Montreal), he plated more than ninety. Dave Bristol, who managed Tony both in the high minors and with the Reds, made the oft-quoted pronouncement that "if the game lasts long enough, Tony will find a way to win it." Perez himself admits to concentrating more fiercely with men on base. Bob Rathgeber quotes an interview with Rose, asking whom he would like to see at the plate with a runner in scoring position and the game on the line. "Perez." " 'More than anyone else on the team?' 'More than anyone else in baseball. . . . ' 'More than yourself?' 'More than myself' " (p. 132).

And Big Doggie did come through with men in scoring position. He knocked in over one thousand runs for the Reds, passing Frank Robinson's mark. In spite of his having been traded at the end of 1976, his total is second only to that of Bench in the history of the team. And some were as dramatic as any Johnny ever hit. Cincinnati will always remember Tony most gratefully for his sudden heroics in the last two games against Boston. Hitless in fifteen at bats, he came alive with home runs in two consecutive appearances, helping to put game number five in the Reds' column. In the final game, with the team trailing 3–0, the Big Dog caught another one with a man on base and started the comeback that led to the city's first World Championship in thirty-five years.

Tony did not become Big Dog just by knocking in runs, some of them vital. He was—and this is why he comes at the end of this roster—the top dog in the clubhouse as well. Let Sparky tell it: "These guys here

[Detroit clubhouse, 1986] get to teasing and knocking one another, and they think they are pretty good. Well, they are OK and they are a fine bunch, but sometimes when they think they're getting really sharp, I wish old Doggie would walk in. He'd eat them alive.

"Needling was the greatest thing that Reds club had, and Tony Perez was number one and no mistake about it. He could hand it out rougher than anyone, and yet somehow he could do it without offending. That team had a lot of leaders. Rose and Morgan were obvious leaders. But only when Perez left did I realize that he was *the* leader. He did the most to keep all those egos in harmony. Doggie could handle them all."

The bulletin board of the Reds' Tampa locker room in March 1987 featured the notice shown here. Though Tony had just moved his own

LOST - DOGGIE TONY
3 LEGS, BLIND IN LEFT EYE, MISSING RIGHT EAR, TAIL BROKEN, RECENTLY CASTRATED... ANSWERS TO NAME OF "LUCKY"

locker in with the coaches, it looked as though some of the players were still responding to the most famous of all needles.

STOWE: "You could walk into that clubhouse and think no one gave a shit for the other guy."

CONCEPCION: "You could call Pete Rose any name you wanted. To Morgan we say, 'Oh, you only good for stealing bases.' To me they say, 'Get away, we talking here about hitting.' "

STOWE: "There was a clear and careful arrangement in the clubhouse right down to the placement of the lockers. Sparky himself instigated much of the needling, even though he seldom participated. He'd call Bench in and say like, 'Why don't you see why Tony's having such a tough time with the foul popups?' And the he'd stand just behind the door and listen."

Sparky broke his own rule when dealing with the hitting drought of Tony Perez through the first four games of the Boston Series. Tom Boswell quotes Anderson: "I told him, 'Doggie, keep it up. Hodges [low watermark for sluggers with disappointing Series] is in sight. Just think, only four more outs and you've set a whole new record.' " Perez responded with a hitting spree that included a pivotal game-tying home run and left him with a Series batting average of .417 (Washington *Post*, 10/5/87, p. C4).

SPARKY: "Oh, I loved to hear those guys carry on. They were just great. I'd put a certain group of them together in a batting-practice sequence and then go up and lean on the cage. I was never disappointed. I always got a good show."

STOWE: "They picked on the younger players, too, made them feel part of the team."

SPARKY: "And Richie Scheinblum never got over being awed by the stars on our team and the way they bantered with each other in the clubhouse, on the bus, and around the batting cage. We unloaded Scheinblum early to the Angels, where presumably he would be unawed" (Anderson and Burick, p. 143). This quotation, taken from Sparky's autobiography, really doesn't sound like him. He ran the gamut from warm to livid, but no one ever accused him of being "snide." On the other hand, the fate of Richie Scheinblum equates with a feeling one gets from listening to Bernie Stowe and some of the more avid needlers: namely, that after an hour of pregame give-and-take, the ballgame itself must have seemed a welcome respite.

CONCEPCION: "Yeah, it could get pretty rough, and sometimes we did kid about who made how much money. Like, 'How come they pay you so much when all you good for is steal bases.' But we can say those things because we are friends. Who know each other's families. We go to each other's houses."

PEREZ: "It was a way to make a long season tolerable and to make everyone a part of the team. A guy makes an error and the next day you put a bucket by his locker. You joke about it, but you don't let him forget it, and maybe he learns a thing or two."

CONCEPCION: "Mostly we didn't pick on guys when they were down. When you use the needle to make a point, you do it when the guy is up."

STOWE: "You'd see rookies come up like Dave Collins and Knight,

Retirement ceremonies for Tony Perez showed appreciation of Big Doggie's prowess with bat and quip as well as Pituka's role of big sister to younger players' wives. (Courtesy Cincinnati Reds)

and they'd just sit in the corner and you'd never know they were there. But if they started getting discouraged and just going through the motions, the regulars wouldn't have that. 'Come on, son, time to get your ass in gear.' And if Sparky ever saw anyone sulking, he'd get him in the office and let him get it off his chest.

"But everybody was on your case. You'd do something and it wasn't twenty minutes later they'd be all over your ass. 'Three-and-two and you were looking for a curve? What's the matter with you, you never saw a low fastball before?' And one would let up and another would take over. Of course they followed every pitch.

"The other side was Morgan or Rose coming back from the plate and telling the next guy what to look for, and this kind of thing was going on all the time. No one realizes how much Perez helped Geronimo as a hitter. When he came up, he was always going for the fences; Doggie taught him to wait, to go with the pitches. You had Tony working with the Latins, Bench helping the young catchers. It was like having a whole other set of coaches."

KLU: "The needling was a teaching device. It was a way of pointing out flaws in a comical, therefore acceptable, way."

SPARKY: "That team was so full of guys that really understood the game! Now Pete is a manager, so everyone thinks he was the smart one, and he was. But Bench and Morgan! They knew the game inside out. Tony did, too, but he is maybe just too nice a guy to be able to be mean to people when he has to. But at least three guys on that team would make first-class managers."

PETE: "Yeah, that's right, the needling was a way to get the point across without being too heavy. The ribbing got rough, but there were no hard feelings. We got along real well, and we stayed together a long time."

Ritter Collet called this "seemingly acrimonious flow of insults" the "glue" that held the stars together. Although it sounds like the beginning of "an impending gang fight," it was for the Reds a "way of life" from which no one was exempt (p. 58).

STOWE: "Yes, I was in on it. Morgan would pick my ass up and toss me in the laundry hamper. Or someone would hang me up by my feet. On the road when they had lockers that didn't reach the ceiling, they'd make me the basketball [Bernie tends toward the spherical] and toss me up there. Did they give me warning so I could take off my glasses? In a pig's ear; but no, they never hurt you. And no, I was hardly silent while this was going on, and yes, I have the vocabulary for it."

SPARKY: "Yes, it was fortunate that the three leaders in all this were black, white, and Latin. But that wasn't necessary to keep down racism. There just wasn't any. Pete and Johnny just don't have a bit of that in them. I mean none. And neither does Joe or his wife, Gloria. I've been to their home and I know both of their parents, and there is just no consciousness of color anywhere in that family. Hell, you bring up black and white with Joe and he laughs at you.

"Joe tried to explain to me why players seem to pair off racially away from the ballpark. This puzzled me for a long time because I knew there was no bias, but yet I seldom saw black and white players together in public. Joe said it was mostly the music; that the players had different tastes; that blacks tended to carry tapes with them, and preferred to listen to particular stations or their own tapes in their hotel rooms. It was more entertaining to them than just sitting around bars, which is what the white players prefer."

The Reds did have problems with black players over the years, well publicized because of the great ability of these athletes: Frank Robinson, Bobby Tolan, George Foster.

KENNEDY: "Robinson was just a bad actor when he was here. He did pull a gun in a restaurant, and that was not all. But I could make you a much longer list of white players who didn't fit in and who were traded or sold. Gene Freese was one; maybe Milt Pappas made as much trouble as any persuading the other pitchers not to throw when the least bit tired or in pain. There were plenty."

STOWE: "Robinson and Pinson were both very self-centered when they came up. It was 'I this and me that.' They both went to the same high school, and it became them against the rest. I was sure it would be Pinson that would be traded, but one of them had to go."

SPARKY: "Well, there was something buried in George Foster. I have no evidence of this, but I always suspected that he had, at some time, been badly mistreated by whites, maybe even before he came to California. But most of the time George got along with everyone just fine."

HOWSAM: "Foster was no problem. Tolan was just a real fine young man who underwent a most unfortunate change of attitude. We avoided problems by getting rid of those types long before they got to the big leagues."

PETE: "Race is no barrier if you are willing to work."

STOWE: "The big thing was it was so much fun. In those days we all took a bus back to the hotel when we are on the road (now everyone goes his own way), and Sparky didn't allow no horsing around if you lost. You couldn't even sneeze. He'd hear some guys laughing in the back of the bus after the other team won and he'd hollar, 'Shut the fuck up! We're losing important games, and you guys think it's funny!'

"But they won so many games and they were such great guys, and they really knew how to dig one another."

SPARKY: "If they hadn't been talented guys with real class they wouldn't have known how to take that stuff. They couldn't have done it."

STOWE: "You know every clubhouse has its clowns: they nail your shoes to the floor or put mentholatum in your jock. Davey is a little like that, always horsing around, and he almost paid for it. In Chicago he climbed in the big clothes dryer and Pat Zachry—probably getting even for something—pushed the button. By the time they stopped it, his hair was already singed and his arms burned.

"But what was special about those guys was not this horseplay. It was the digging; you had to be able to go with it or you were in trouble."

Apparently a goodly portion of the raillery had to do with sickness and injuries and whether or not you were going to let them keep you out of the lineup. This was the theme of everyone's favorite episode, possibly because one of the chief verbal aggressors was himself the victim. Every single player who was there—and some who weren't—mentioned it. The manager seems to have relished it as much as anyone.

SPARKY: "We were playing New York, and Jerry Koosman was due to pitch, and he was really good in those days: tough on left-handers. Morgan was sick; had a temperature over 102 degrees, and I had him scratched from the lineup. Suddenly I hear all this laughter from the locker room, and they come and get me. In front of Morgan's locker they've stretched out a sleeping bag, a pillow, a glass of water, some aspirin. Maybe there was even a wheelchair, I don't know. But there was a big sign: 'Take these pills and get plenty of bedrest. Tomorrow you'll be over your attack of Koosmanitis.'

"I went back in my office, and soon I hear screaming; Morgan comes tearing into my office. 'What is all this shit? I'm playing!' 'No, you're not, I told him, 'you've got a fever and you're out of the lineup.' "The hell I am. I'm not going to let that Cuban son-of-a-bitch get me this time. I'm playing if I have to tear this place apart!' So I had to put Joe back in the lineup."

STOWE: "And he went ofer [got no hits], and then they started ragging him about being tired."

ROBINSON: "A winning team comes from more than raw talent. It takes interaction, though you can't always tell what kind.

"With the Orioles we had the Kangaroo Court. Frank [Robinson] was a judge with arbitrary powers who made comical awards and assessed fines. The court was a way of softening the abrasive personality of the natural team leader. It combined ridicule with humor; the result was team feeling.

"In general, the Reds' rumpus room had the same traits. Critical remarks were softened with humor. The result was closer team feeling.

"That may be a thing of the past. Today you can't kid people because you don't know who's on drugs or what. You have to watch your step. This atmosphere, together with the fact that the players all have their own agents, has changed team dynamics; or, you might say, you have less of a team and more today a collection of individuals."

The needle pricks in more ways than one, and there are, inevitably, cases where the wound gets infected. One case involved Sparky's favorite coach and sidekick, George Scherger, whom Sparky credits with teaching him more than any other person about the work and concentration necessary for victory. Scherger's strong point was the game's fundamentals, and he was a hard taskmaster. As a way of getting back at the disciplinarian, some of the team started teasing him about his own lack of major-league experience, which was total. George took it for a while and then . . .

SPARKY: "Yeah, old Sugar had enough. He was going to fight. He was going to let them know he wasn't taking it anymore, and if we hadn't stopped him there would have been one helluva fight."

Another infectious case was that of Bobby Tolan, who was an outstanding centerfielder for the Reds from 1969 to 1973. He had physical problems, seemingly accompanied by a change of attitude. Since injuries were fair game in that clubhouse, Tolan, recovering from a snapped achilles tendon and suffering from back problems, became a special target. Sparky was in a dilemma. If he told the players to ease up, he would be isolating the target. So he had to let it go on and, in Bernie Stowe's words, "Tolan just snapped. The needling turned him into a loner. He couldn't take it, and you couldn't be a loner on that ballclub." Sparky, in his autobiography, calls his handling of Tolan his biggest mistake; to me he said, "If I could have just spent more time with him, I could have seen this coming and headed it off."

The needling and still another injury had a lot to do with putting the Big Red Machine into overdrive. The 1975 season saw the Reds off to a good start, then stumbling in their second series against the Dodgers. After winning a few, the Reds lost four straight in Philadelphia. Pete Rose had been moved to third, John Vukovich dismissed, George Foster installed in left, and Rawley Eastwick called up from Indianapolis. But these vital shifts had not taken their eventual toll, and Manager Anderson was afraid that the habitual hard clubhouse digging was unsettling the younger players and helping no one. A ceasefire was imposed, to no apparent avail. Moving to Montreal on May 18, the Reds lost still another game, six in a row, dropping them below .500. Moreover, a hard slide into second had ripped open Morgan's shin, cutting down to the bone.

The clubhouse the next day was as low as it had ever been when suddenly Morgan, fresh from the doctor, burst in grinning and shouting profanities left and right. "Fuck you, Rose," he challenged, "and you, too," he added looking right at Anderson. "And are you ever going to hit a homer again, Perez?" "And are you going to let that little scratch keep you out of the game?" shot back Doggie. Suddenly the ceasefire is over, the whole clubhouse is rocking. Morgan plays with fourteen fresh stitches; the ban on the bantering is lifted. The Reds begin one of the most intimidating winning streaks in modern baseball (see chapter five). The Big Red Machine was laying its patch (Hertzel, pp. 75–76, plus interviews).

STOWE: "Sparky told me in spring training of '75, 'We're going to win it this year.' The next year he told me, 'We're goin' to repeat.' And as those years went on, you could begin to feel the spirit grow. They were all yelling at each other, picking each other up, letting no one forget. They'd complain about the ballpark in Pittsburgh. They didn't like the field or something. 'Let's not have to come back here again,' they'd say, and they'd win in three. Then in New York in '76 after the third game, it was kind of cold and unpleasant. 'We don't want to have to sit out in that lousy Yankee weather again, do we? Come on, let's wrap it up.' And you knew that they would. They were really something.

"And there was only one manager who could've handled them in that way—letting them have their head but somehow planning it all and keeping control—and that was Sparky."

Tom Seaver didn't get to know Sparky until he was well along in his career, but he came to like him almost immediately when he received an unqualified welcome on joining the Reds from the Mets. Respect came later for this man whom Seaver found acting "crazy" half the time and getting himself worked up by his own dugout oratory. Seaver makes fun of Sparky for exaggerating his own professional career, but he found Anderson intelligent, open-minded, yet a firm believer in his own convictions. "He'll argue to the death when he thinks he's right. And usually he is right" (Anderson and Burick, p. 218).

Johnny Bench realized, after the Series debacle in 1970, that Sparky would mean something special to the club. He began calling him "John," after John McGraw, because of his will to win, his strong determination,

Sparky Anderson uses the full range of emotions to get the best from his players. TOP: Sparky reveals his nearly paternal affection for Dave Concepcion. (Courtesy *Cincinnati Enquirer*) BOTTOM: Sparky's temper, once his worst enemy, can still motivate. (Courtesy Cincinnati Reds)

and his many moves. He found Anderson approachable; as one student of the game to another, Bench would often debate moves and policies. There were few disagreements, none of long standing. After eight years, Bench "wouldn't want to play for anyone else. . . . he has handled a bunch of stars and kept us all at our proper level. . . . he is our leader" (Anderson and Burick, p. 95).

Joe Morgan, too, appreciates Sparky's openness, his willingness to talk things out. He wants to win and encourages aggressive but not vicious tactics—a point concerning which Joe and George have disagreed. In the end, Joe found the manager "more special" than any of the star players. The success of the team revolves around its sometimes self-effacing manager, Joe concluded. "And the longer I stay with this club, the more important I realize that he is to us" (Anderson and Burick, p. 120).

George Lee Anderson was born in Bridgewater, South Dakota, but moved with his parents to Los Angeles when he was nine years old. He remembers a realtor who used a deprecatory term referring to blacks while showing houses to the Andersons. Mrs. Anderson told him she did not want to hear that word again. George grew up in a white neighborhood not far from Watts. You didn't cross the residential color line unless it was for gang fights, recalls Sparky, with no great feeling about the seriousness of such encounters. His favorite playmate was black, and his all-out sports hero was Joe Louis.

Sparky, a convert to Romann Catholicism, became seriously interested in baseball through the attentions of a Jewish part-time scout named Harold Ross "Lefty" Phillips, one of the earliest of Sparky's many intense loyalties. Phillips got him a bid from the Dodgers, which the Andersons allowed him to accept even though he had another, more lucrative proposition.

Loyalty is one key to Sparky's character. He gives it, once it has been earned, without stint and holds onto it tenaciously. It is visible in his dedication to mentors, coaches, and players alike. He clearly expects it in return. When Don Gullett, the kid pitcher from the small town in Kentucky, chose to leave the Reds for the Yankees and a fat contract, Sparky termed it a "defection." Sparky had given Gullett his full support; and, after all, had not he himself given up a higher price tag in order to express his fealty to Lefty Phillips? Sparky is still overtly loyal to Cincinnati, to the team executives of his era, and to his former players. There is no doubt that he is commensurately bitter about the lack of loyalty shown in his dismissal.

Another key to the Spark is plainness. He seems to have no prejudices, nor is he impressed by class or status. Although a careful dresser, he prefers to avoid the trendy spots and seeks not the company of the rich and famous. He has no side. His friends are the ordinary people he meets in the course of his job: workers, mechanics, ticket-takers. His idea of recreation is a day of fishing in relaxed company or a Sunday chicken dinner with a folksy family.

These traits should not be confused with passivity or ignorance. George Anderson is bright, observant, involved, and determined. He had to study hard in order to master his own fierce temper. Even now, by his own admission, he tends to get involved in too many issues. Coach Kluzewski once counseled him to be more selective; to make sure a question was important before he attacked it. This he has learned to do, to a degree. Feeling that hard work holds the answer to most questions, he has also learned to restrain the pace at which he works his athletes.

When George Anderson became the Reds' manager in 1970, he walked into an operation that was being very carefully defined by Bob Howsam and his staff. He had to accept a roster and a way of doing things that he might not have chosen or designed himself. While being perfectly loyal to his employers, Anderson was also able to convince the players that he was no front-office puppet. That he was his own man. From that point on, says Pete Rose, there were no problems. He let the players have fun. But when the situation calls for it, he will "chew hell out of all of us," says Pete. "He's pretty good at that, too" (Anderson and Burick, p. 65).

The star players liked Sparky because he did not seem to threaten their egos with his own. He had learned the hard way to be even-tempered, but he left no doubt that he was in charge and asserted himself loudly and profanely when he felt the need. There was no soft spot in his will to win. He sought victory not so much through a Napoleonic type of leadership as through the creation of a subtle, complex network within which individuals were encouraged to have their own ideas. Above all, he gave and expected loyalty. With Sparky's future on the line, Pete Rose was quoted as saying, "I'd go through hell in a gasoline suit for him" (*Cincinnati Post*, 10/2/78, p. 23).

The Reds of the 1970s were memorable for their six division titles, four National League pennants, and two consecutive World Series victories. They are memorable to Bernie Stowe because they were "a helluva bunch of guys," digging and helping one another, having a great time and winning so many games. They are memorable to Johnny Bench because, like his high school basketball team in Binger, they had a special "karma," each playing on the best abilities of the other and knowing exactly what they were. They were memorable according to Bob Howsam because they possessed, as a group, that energy that enables a team to play beyond what it thinks it can do and realize its true destiny.

They did this, in part, by exercising a form of bantering communication that was deliberately disrespectful, harsh at times, universally profane, and constructive only when applied to the task at hand. Had this style anything to do with the part of the country the Reds represented? Bernie Stowe thinks it does. Perhaps the South is more formal, New England more laconic, and the West Coast more laid back. Surely it is common in the Midwest to greet an old friend with a string of insulting profanity and to have this taken as a form of affection.

Cussing and cutting up one another is a property of team sports everywhere, and it would be silly to insist that locker-room banter was the singular property of any team, region, or game. Yet it is clear that this team somehow developed this technique into an art form: a form that assisted palpably in expressing loyalties and enforcing teamwork. The Big Red Machine won ballgames on the field, in part, because of their skilled and instructive use of the needle. In perfecting this technique, they were led by their cagey tactician and field boss, George Lee Anderson, who rightly titled his autobiography *The Main Spark*.

Chapter Five.....
THE REDS PLAYERS
On Stage at Riverfront

HOWSAM: "Your ballpark is a stage. People sit there for three hours watching a show. The players are the actors: that's what they are, actors in uniform. The producers are the coaches and managers throughout the system. It is up to them to make the actors perform well."

The drama critic in reviewing the performances at Riverfront during the 1970s would be interested in a number of questions. How important was the artificial ground cover? Were these teams assembled with the carpet particularly in mind? Did they, in any way, pioneer in introducing a new kind of tactical game tailored to this surface? Had this company of players, at home or touring, any special strengths? How important were the stars as opposed to the supporting cast? When at the top of their form, did they have any distinguishing traits?

HOWSAM: "Artificial turf is great. It allows baseball to be played the way it should be played. You get only true bounces. You can't doctor the infield by tilting the baselines or letting the grass grow too long. The carpet allowed a good shortstop like Woody Woodward to make the occasional great play. All of this tends to make close plays, and that's what the fans like.

"The carpet is important in other ways. It avoids rainouts. One year we figure the carpet saved us twenty-seven, twenty-nine games. That year we had 2.7 million attendance.

"But aside from the saved revenue, the saved games allow a good team to retain momentum. Postponed games tend to hurt a good team, on a streak, and to let a lesser team pull itself together. So for this reason, too, the carpet tended to abet the Reds of the seventies."

SPARKY: "Turf makes a difference. It is *great* for base-stealing. You get a good start. You won't slip or spin your wheels. Great traction.

"You get true bounces. Had Mazeroski played on the carpet, he'd never made an error. I played second and I can tell. A player with good hands ought never miss a ball on turf.

"On the carpet the whole thing is speed. Speed's the whole thing: stealing bases and defense.

"But you see I'm not a carpet man. I think when you're playing on the carpet you're playing a different ballgame. It's hard on the legs. A guy that plays through a long career on the artificial turf is much more likely to have leg injuries. It tears up the legs. You have troubles when you get older.

"Playing on the turf is not baseball, it's something else; or at least it is a different form of the game."

Walter Langsam argues that Riverfront Stadium was not suited to the Cincinnati ballclub and in support points out that it took almost three years, after the opening of Riverfront, for the Reds' home record to equal their road record. Until then, the carpet had favored the visitor.

CONCEPCION: "We didn't make innovations in playing baseball on the artificial turf. Other teams (Houston, St. Louis) had been there before and adjusted.

"But the adjustment took a while. We had to discover, for example, that the ball bounces different between day and night, when the surface is hot or cool, wet or dry.

"As for the one-bounce throw to first, you couldn't do that on grass."

KLU: "You adjust to the artificial surface easily. Sure it's different; but you play a few games and there you are. What took a lot of adjusting was from Crosley to Riverfront. It is just a different experience altogether.

"Crosley Field was, like this city, small and friendly. Hell, I made most of my friends at the ballpark. Now here, in these large cement stadiums, you can't even hear what people in the stands are saying. I mean that literally. The acoustics are so bad at Riverfront that you have to step out of the dugout even to hear what's coming over the public-address speakers.

"Playing on the carpet is, with some variations, like playing anywhere, and the key to winning is the same. Your farm system brings you up accomplished players, trained to play your kind of ball, and you win. Otherwise forget it."

Then, seeming to argue against himself, Ted Kluzewski began speculating as to whether his teammate shortstop Roy McMillan—whom many consider to have been among the game's very best—could have played on artificial turf. "He had a better arm than either Ozzie Smith or Concepcion, but he didn't have their range." When Mac's prowess was defended Klu backed down a bit, but insisted, "Mac might've had a little trouble on the turf. He would've had to learn even more about playing position on each hitter and each pitch."

PEREZ: "The Reds of the seventies would have won on any surface. The trading for speed was just because the game had changed."

KENNEDY: "They'll *tell* you they put together a team for the carpet."

BELL: "A lot of the teams with artificial turf stressed speed. This was partly because they also had bigger ballparks. The Reds of the seventies were fast, quick, and hit. They could do anything you asked them to. Tremendous. Could have played anywhere: yeah, could have won on Mars."

WELSH: "Were the Reds innovators of carpet baseball? Just the opposite. I was playing college and amateur ball and coming to understand tactics. It would drive me crazy how the Reds would overlook basic tactics: the sacrifice, the hit-and-run."

SPARKY: "Yeah, you're right. I was never one for deliberately wasting an out. You only get twenty-seven in a normal game, and you may need them all. Why give them away? With this Detroit team I have to 'play the percentages' a little more because it's that kind of ballclub. But with the Reds we could afford to use all our outs."

WELSH: "But they were innovative on defense: Joe and David, anyway."

PARKER: "Howsam showed that you could win with speed. Herzog got the credit for it, but Howsam showed it. On defense Morgan and Concepcion were innovative, kind of, but so was Chuck Tanner."

PETE: "We weren't pioneers on the turf, we were just good. The trade to get Morgan improved the team because he is so smart and because it gave the team more than one way to win."

ROBINSON: "Speed goes with astroturf. Look at Kansas City. For years they used to drive the Orioles crazy in their own park. They had adjusted and we hadn't.

"You can run better, steal more bases. Outfield hits head more quickly for the gaps, where speed is needed to cut them off. It speeds up the whole game.

"The bounces are so true—although different for each surface—that it gives the fielder a feeling of invincibility. Yet it is harder for a player who plays mostly on grass to adjust to the carpet than vice versa.

"Defense is getting to the ball and catching it. On the carpet, catching it is relatively easy; so you can afford to put the emphasis on getting to it. Infielders and outfielders play deeper, needing to cover more ground. Speed again.

"Speed is getting to be everything. Hell, today I probably wouldn't even've been signed!"

The stress on speed, like much else in modern baseball, goes back to Branch Rickey. Rickey could and did explain why speed was so vital.

Compared at least to baseball's other skills, speed is unteachable; throwing may be nearly as innate. Therefore, the scouts and the minor-league managers look for and develop speed and throwing above all other basic attributes in the rising players. Howsam knew "Mr. Rickey," as everyone called him, respected his teachings, and does not at all mind being called a disciple.

KLU: "The policy became: 'If you can't run and throw, we don't want you.' Where does this leave the hitting coach? I am looking at a team of rifle-armed jockeys. Everyone is 5'9". For goodness sake, where are the hitters? I want to scream, 'Bring me up someone who can hit the ball!'

"You know the team today makes the same mistakes we made in the earlier days. Everyone makes these mistakes. The pitcher gets wild. You kick a ball or two. It always happens. But the difference between now and then was *we had the bop!*

"We would make the same mistakes, then *bam bam bam:* five runs. When you have the hitting, you can always come back. This 1986 team has trouble making up even one run."

If there is one thing the Reds did on defense that was distinctive of play on the artificial turf, it was, all agree, the one-bounce throw to first. Shortstop David Concepcion tried it when suffering from a sore arm. He stuck with it. When forced deep in the hole by a ground ball, he would pivot while releasing a throw aimed about four feet short of the bag. The first baseman took it on a rising hop.

CONCEPCION: "I didn't invent that throw. I saw another fellow do it. I saw Brooks Robinson do it to Lee May here in 1971. Then when my arm was hurt, I decided why not try it."

ROBINSON: "I remember that throw. It was the only way I was going to get the ball to first on that play. You couldn't do it on grass, but on the carpet it is not a bad play [said with admiration]."

KATZ: "A couple of physicists set up a test on that kind of throw. They showed scientifically that the bounced throw takes longer to reach the object. Pete told Davey not to do it anymore."

CONCEPCION: "I don't think that's right. The ball picks up speed when it hits the turf. It is coming up while the thrown ball is dying. It gives less chance of an error and more chance for the out."

PETE: "David made that throw at first because he had to. It doesn't pick up speed unless the turf is wet. Then it does. It doesn't lose speed unless it hits in the dirt right in front of the bag. So long as you bounce it far enough out, on the carpet, it is OK."

CONCEPCION: "No, Pete never tell me not to throw it. I did it a couple times this summer. I did it last week in Philadelphia. It worked."

A premier shortstop of the 1970s, here Concepcion is about to release his patented one-bounce throw to first. (Courtesy Cincinnati Reds)

ROBINSON: "The ball doesn't speed up any, but it will kind of scoot on the turf. It avoids the risk of an overthrow, even if you don't get the runner."

HOWSAM: "The bounced throw will pick up speed if it has overspin. Mr. Rickey taught that."

KLU: "There's nothing wrong with catching a throw on the bounce once you get used to the way the infielder throws it. Everyone puts his own type spin on the ball, and it can surprise you. But once you get used to it, there's no difference from catching it on the fly. In fact it might be better to have the ball coming up at you."

WELSH: "Those teams were innovative on defense."

One of the clichés of baseball is strength up the middle. Although the catcher, second baseman, shortstop, and centerfielder have to handle the bat, the concept is basically one of defense.

Pitching is part of the middle, of course, but a strong catcher helps that. In a game where most balls are hit back the way they came, it is helpful to have fielders who can get to them and make the plays. If there was any trait where the Big Red Machine showed true dominance, it was in strength up the middle.

The Reds' pitching during these years may have been given an undeservedly bad name. But it probably would not create any argument to assert that the Reds' pitching of the 1970s was not intimidating. The defense, however, was. It made up for the absence of a Bob Gibson or a Sandy Koufax.

Consider the plight of the opposing hitter. A left-handed pull hitter gets his pitch and starts it toward the hole. Morgan, with the quickest of first steps, has seen the catcher's sign, has anticipated the characteristic pull, and has cut the ball off at ankle level, back to the bag. He has plenty of time to turn and lob to first.

Timing the pitch squarely, the next batter grounds one through the box; but this just gives Concepcion the chance for his top move: a glide to his left so quick and smooth it seems but a single step. In fact, he meets the ball not just in the outfield but often on the rightfield side of the bag! There, taking the ball on a high hop, Davey draws back his right shoulder against the grain of the move, and slings—rather than throws, and often off the wrong foot—an unerring dart to Doggie.

Catching the ball on the fat part of the bat gives another hitter a fine long drive to the gap. Will it be in for two or three? Even the accustomed fan may wonder as Geronimo, moving before the spectator's eye can find him, begins his seemingly leisurely move to intersect the flight of the ball.

It looks like the ball will drop. But the estimate has not included the abnormally long stride of the "Chief," whose effortless canter, now turned toward a gallop, eats the acres of center field with an ease that belies the vision. At hip-height, the triple surrenders to the outstretched glove.

Later in the game, frustrated by a robbery or two, the swifter batters try to lay one down. Now it is the turn of the sizeable Bench to transform himself into a cat as abruptly as Geronimo became a thoroughbred. The mask flies, the overdeveloped haunches propel the catcher into fair territory with startling suddenness. The oversized right hand grips the ball and pulls it back to the ear. Then comes the unparalleled quick release and level throw, chest high, to the inside corner of the bag. Done. 2–3.

To praise the middle defense of the Big Red Machine is not to speculate but to recognize a judgment already firmly in place. Of this awesome defense, Johnny Bench was first on the scene, winning a Gold Glove in 1968. He won the award for being the best defensive catcher in the National League the next year and the year after. He won for *ten* consecutive years. Pete Rose won twice, as an outfielder in '69 and '70; Tommy Helms won Gold Gloves at second base for the Reds in '70 and '71.

Morgan won his first of five awards in 1973. The next year he was joined by Concepcion and Geronimo. *Then for four consecutive years, 1974–1977, the Reds won Gold Gloves at all four middle positions: Bench, Morgan, Concepcion, and Geronimo.* It is frequently pointed out that the Reds had an "elegant" defense, or that they won over twenty-five Gold Gloves in the 1970s. But the basic strength of this club was its defensive prowess up the vital spine of the diamond.

SPARKY: "Yes, indeed, we had strength up the middle. Every one of those Reds was number one at his position.

"I have been very fortunate. I have had two teams that were very strong up the middle [referring then to the Tigers featuring Parrish, Trammel, Whitaker, and Lemon]. I think these were the two best teams up the middle I've ever seen. But I would have to admit that the Tigers were a notch below the Reds in both offense and defense."

HOWSAM: "Concepcion is as good a shortstop as I've ever seen."

"The Trade" had a lot to do with middle strength in ways that are not always appreciated. It is hard to overestimate the importance of Joe Morgan; yet Morgan's strength was in his total contribution. Howsam calls him the best all-round offensive player he's ever seen. Defensively he may not have added that much to a team that traded away a two-time Gold Glove second baseman as part of the deal. It is fair to say that the Trade contributed the most to defensive strength in the acquisition of Cesar Geronimo, whom Ritter Collett calls the "perfect" outfielder for

This blurred image suggests Johnny Bench's speed in reacting to a topped ball in front of the plate. (Courtesy Cincinnati Reds)

TOP: Posing with the glove manufacturer's representative at the annual award ceremony are, *left to right*, Gold Glove winners Johnny Bench, Dave Concepcion, Cesar Geronimo, and Joe Morgan. (Courtesy Cincinnati Reds) BOTTOM: The Reds' "controlled arrogance" shows in this almost bored contratulatory round after their opening victory over the Yankees in 1976. *Left to right*, Bench, Concepcion, Perez, Morgan, Rose, and relief pitcher Pedro Borbon. (Courtesy *Cincinnati Enquirer*)

the large, modern center fields. His long stride and deceptive speed gave him the essential coverage; he had the arm for a brisk 200-foot throw to the cut-off man, or, from closer in, for making a close play at any base (p.215).

To stress the middle is not to ignore the edges. No one does. It would be impossible to overlook Pete Rose, coming up as a peppery second baseman, then shifting to the outfield where he trademarked the technique of deliberately running under a catch in order to create momentum for the throw. Playing either first or third, Rose challenged would-be bunters by seeming to creep close enough to read their watches.

Griffey had blinding speed and a fine arm in right; Foster, when he wanted to, could run, catch, and throw with the best.

Yet day in, day out, nothing supports a team like its backbone through the middle of the diamond. It makes strong pitching invincible. It makes average pitching strong. It may even make intolerable pitching tolerable.

Was the Big Red Machine the best defensive team of all time? Such a claim, seldom made, would be hard to support. It would, on the other hand, be hard to find another team whose four central positions produced sixteen Gold Gloves in four years.

BENCH: "The Reds did not teach the league how to play on the carpet, but they refined this kind of baseball. We played the game right."

PETE: "The Reds of the seventies were just good. It was a good trade to get Morgan, the most intelligent ballplayer I ever played with. Didn't play deeper than anyone else, just played smarter."

SPARKY: "There were at least three players on that team that knew all about baseball: knew enough to make first-rate managers. Morgan is extremely intelligent, but he is into too many things. You'd have to lock him up in a room to make him a manager. Bench understands the game as well as anyone, but he'd rather have his own life, play golf and so forth, and now he's getting more into announcing. And Pete studies the game more relentlessly than anyone.

"I predict Pete will break my records as Reds manager: most games won and longevity."

If you said to a fan, "Joe Morgan sure is one smart ballplayer," the reply would be something like: "Oh yeah. He studies those pitchers until he can read their moves like large print. Never gets picked off; rarely thrown out." And yet, in his *Baseball My Way*, Morgan spends even more space on defensive positioning than on keys to pitchers' deliveries. To say that Morgan is a student of the game is to commit an understatement. In words and in deeds he is, furthermore, a demonstration that smart baseball does not mean any single aspect of the game (Morgan, pp. 30–37).

The notation 9–2 in a scorecard usually means the rightfielder threw out a runner at home. Occasionally the Reds gave it a different meaning.

Morgan has a play on the ball, but it gets through the hole, the second baseman's momentum carrying him over toward the foul line. Perez, naturally, drifts toward the outfield to take the throw. Bench, off with the runner, begins to make the defensive catcher's V with the first-base line, putting him in position to backstop first on a throw from the infield.

All quiet. Routine single. The batter makes a wide turn at first and, seeing Perez in front of him, takes a generous piece of the baseline toward second.

Suddenly something changes. Bench has abandoned his trot toward the coaching box, dropped the mask, and sprinted toward first. The coach hollers, "Heads up!" but it is too late. The rightfielder (notably Rose before the shift), having cocked his arm preparing a routine throw to the cut-off, suddenly pivots and unleashes a clothesline to the first bag. Catcher and ball arrive together, two steps ahead of the betrayed base-runner. A thumb is raised. One out, man on first has become two out, bases empty.

BENCH: "The thing is that every time I made that cut and ran for the bag, the throw would be there. The throw would be there at the perfect time. I always knew it would be.

"Those Reds were like my Binger [Oklahoma] High School basketball team. Five of us played together from the sixth grade on. We never had to look for a teammate, we knew where everyone was. Those teams had a karma, a rapport that allowed them to make the unusual play.

"This karma gave us [the Reds] what I call inner conceit. We didn't come to the ballpark hoping to win, we came knowing we would win."

SPARKY: "Those guys used to irk me and I'd say, 'You guys think you're so good you can turn it off and on at will!' And they could."

BENCH: "We were so good the other teams would stay out to watch us take infield and batting practice."

Rose, with the Reds two runs down coming into the ninth, would holler, "All right, we've got 'em right where we want 'em!"

Sometimes this confidence coupled with the demonstrated ability to come from behind could have an impact. Hal McCoy points to a series in Houston, June 30–July 2, 1975. The Reds had won every game coming from behind or in extra innings or both. Slated to pitch the finale, Joe Niekro quipped: "I'm here to sweep the series!" The jest was only half a joke. Seeing the tenacity and variety of the Reds' attack, some teams seemed to lose a bit of their will to win against the "machine."

McCoy insists that the true trademark of the 1975 champion team was the variety of ways it could find to win. There was no small circle of heroes. The point is borne out by the fact that only one Red has ever led the league in game-winning runs batted in. Many fans would miss a lot of guesses as to his identity before coming up with Dave Concepcion.

The last game of the 1975 season was a case in point. Down several times, the home team—despite a makeshift lineup and a lead of some twenty games over the second-place Dodgers—kept coming back. By the last of the ninth, the game was tied. Back-up catcher Bill Plummer, not the speediest of the Reds, nevertheless managed to plate the winning marker without the aid of a hit.

The third baseman's boot put Plummer on first; a passed ball got him to second. He took third on a fielder's choice, whence he scored on a high-bouncing infield grounder off the bat of Geronimo. (That was only the Chief's fifty-third RBI for the season.) Just like the whole season, quips McCoy: winning with whatever, however, and whoever was needed (p. 14).

SPARKY: "I'll never forget, we went into Los Angeles once three games behind the Dodgers. Pete says, 'The Dodgers are in first place chasin' us.' It made the headlines. Pete always knew just when to say what."

In the first decade of Riverfront, the Reds dominated their league as have few other teams in the history of the game. One way to summarize this superiority is through numbers, games won and lost, overall percentages, composite standings. But numbers alone suggest an impersonal piece of machinery. On the other hand, each roster, each series, even single games and innings had their special personalities. Each tells something about the character of the team and its constituent parts.

If you ask some of the older Reds, including their manager of that era, about the outstanding teams, they will start by reminding you of the early part of the decade, in particular the Reds of 1970 and 1972, which they remember as the teams with the most "pure muscle," the impressive ability to pound the long ball. It was actually the late sixties when the lineup including Pete Rose, Lee May, Tony Perez, Bobby Tolan, and Johnny Bench began to bombard the fences of old Crosley Field with a regularity that suggested a piece of slugging machinery. The 1970 version was the cream of this crop, winning 102 games in the regular season and shutting out Pittsburgh in the playoffs behind Nolan, Merritt, and Wilcox, before falling victim to the Orioles and Brooks Robinson's magnetic glove.

Mark Schmetzer, in a feature article in the December 20, 1986, *Redsvue*, makes a case for the eminence of the '75 team, not because it won so many games, second in league history, but because it was more human than the juggernaut of 1976. To Schmetzer, being human means being erratic, although it is hard to picture a team being inconsistent while winning 108 games.

Schmetzer reminds his readers that this winner of the thrilling Series over Boston did not start out like a world beater. As of May 20 they were playing only .500 ball and trailed the Dodgers by 5 1/2 games. This was a week after Rose had moved to third. For some reason (see chapter 4), the machine went into high gear at just this time, and for the next 50 games they were one of the best teams ever to play the game.

They won 41 of those games. Billingham, Kirby, and Gullett pitched to a combined 17–0 mark, and left the Dodgers 12 1/2 games behind. During this streak Rose had seventy hits, Morgan batted .351 including nine game-winning RBIs, Bench hit twelve homers and drove in forty-seven runs, while the new leftfielder, Foster, batted .308 with nine homers and four GWRBIs. In the course of the outburst, this team with the "rookie" at third set a league record for defense: 15 consecutive errorless games.

Hal McCoy also pointed to this fifty-game orgy of victory as *the moment* when this Team of the seventies truly asserted itself. What set it off was not only the famous move of Rose to third base but also the establishment of George Foster as a regular and the addition of Rawley Eastwick to the relief corps (p. 12).

Inspired by this incredible streak, the Reds went on to clinch the pennant at the earliest date ever, September 7. They led the league in runs, stolen bases, fewest errors, and saves. In extra-inning games they were 11–4. Moreover, they finished twenty games ahead of a team whose records for runs and hits allowed, and for team earned-run average (2.92), are still the lowest in the books.

These numbers are hard to resist. If sustained winning play is the hallmark, then the 1975 team, in the weeks before the All Star break, was probably the Big Red Machine at its most menacing.

If you ask the players about the high point of the seventies, the answer comes very quickly: winning the World Series in 1975. More so than in 1976? Pete Rose: "There are no words to describe the thrill of winning your first World Championship." The manner in which it was won over the tenacious Red Sox, who seemed to forget that it was Cincinnati who supposedly had a patent on coming from behind, may have added to the luster. No doubt coming from behind one last time on October 22, to win the game and the Series 4–3, made everything just a bit more glowing. But Rose seemed to speak for all the players in stressing the first championship above all else, regardless of how it was achieved.

Were it not for the recognition that goes with the ultimate crown, however, both players and management might vote for the playoff win over Philadelphia in 1976 as the toughest hurdle and the most satisfying postseason triumph.

SPARKY: "The climax for us was in 1976. We beat Carlton and a tough Philadelphia team and then beat the Yankees. No team will ever again sweep postseason play."

HOWSAM: "The culmination of our effort came in 1976, a record for all time. Beating Philadelphia was more of an achievement than beating New York; but we did it, and we did it in style. They said we didn't have any pitching, and we won seven in a row. Somebody had to be throwing the ball, right?"

There is little wonder as to why the Phils were respected. The batting order began with Cash, Maddox, Schmidt, Luzinski, and Richie Allen. The middle was anchored by Boone behind the plate and Bowa at short. The starting pitchers the Reds would face were Carlton, Lomborg, and Kaat. To top it off, Danny Ozark had just been voted Manager of the Year.

The series opened ominously in unfriendly Veterans Stadium, with the home team scoring a run and the visitors' star hurler walking three. Don Gullett, however, regained his control and pitched eight innings without allowing a further score. Three extra-base hits by Rose and a timely double by the pitcher helped build a healthy lead; and the Reds won 6–3 despite two last-of-the-ninth tallies off reliever Eastwick.

The turning point of the series came in the sixth inning of the second game. Till then Jim Lomborg had held the Reds team hitless while the Phils scored twice, one coming on a 500-foot rocket by Greg Luzinski. It was getting toward those late innings that the Reds thought they owned. They started pushing, and, with aggressive baserunning playing its typical part, the momentum of the game turned obligingly around.

Dave Concepcion walked. With pinch-hitter Dan Driessen at the plate, Davey took off for second on an attempted steal. Driessen's infield grounder, otherwise a double play, moved the runner to second. Rose ended the no-hitter driving in Concepcion. Griffey followed with a single to center and Rose, challenging the arm of Maddox, slid headfirst and untouched into third while Griffey took second.

Gene Garber replaced Lomburg at this point and was ordered to walk Morgan intentionally. What happened next happened very quickly—too quickly for the official scorer, thought some—and caused the series' only controversy. Joe Morgan took one of his outrageous leads off first. With the bases loaded and the right-handed slugger Perez at bat, first baseman Allen was playing deep and in the hole. Joe's lead, however, had triggered a pick-off move by Allen. Garber, ignoring Allen, went to the plate, and Perez lined a screamer down the first-base line. Allen, who said he never saw the ball but reacted by instinct, gloved the liner but had to watch it roll beyond him as two runs scored. That was the ballgame and, to all intents, the series. The controversy was over the error assigned to Allen, which some thought unmerited. The important point was that timely hitting and aggressive baserunning had unnerved another adversary.

The ability of the Reds to change the course of a game through constant pressure on the bases had been illustrated even more clearly the year before, in the League Championship Series against the Pirates. This time the turning point seemed to come in the very first game. Pittsburgh had scored two runs in the second and was leading 2–1 as the Reds came to bat in the last of the third. The inning opened with a walk to Joe Morgan, an event so common that his career total of 1,865 is a number surpassed only by Babe Ruth and Ted Williams. Although it was common enough, a walk to the Reds' second-sacker could be an invitation to disaster.

Joe takes his familiar lead, knees slightly bent, arms relaxed, hands extended just beyond the knees, weight carefully balanced. The physical technique Morgan carefully describes in *Baseball My Way*. In the season just concluded, this technique had produced sixty-seven thefts in seventy-seven attempts.

Even more crucial than the physical alertness is the concentration on the pitcher. At this moment Morgan is studying a square-shouldered southpaw listed at 6'5", 215 pounds, who appeared even larger. He has started this opening game because of eighteen wins and a 2.54 ERA. His record, and that of the Pirates, impresses Morgan. He figures the Reds need every edge to beat them.

Eyes intent on Jerry Reuss, Joe Morgan sidles ever farther off first base. Without moving his body, Reuss feints with head and neck, glancing quickly toward Willie Stargell holding the corner. Joe doesn't budge. A left-hander, Reuss has a full view of the first-base drama from his stretch; but Joe also has a full view of Reuss as he awaits the eventual cue—the bend of the knee, the closing of hip or shoulder that commits the throw toward home. Until then, coiled for a spring back to first, Joe inches ever farther toward second.

This is more than the usual battle between pitcher and runner, catcher and manager. Joe had foreseen, well before the results were in, that a strong-hitting Pittsburgh team, with underrated pitching, would win its division. Looking ahead, he persuaded Sparky to adjust the batting order out of respect for the Pirates' strong left-handed pitching. Joe also held special meetings with the team's fastest runners (Foster, Griffey, Concepcion: "Morgan's rabbits," they were sometimes called).

Joe was not trying for a spring clinic in the early fall. He was trying, with his manager's blessing, to persuade his teammates that they could, if they learned how to study the Pirate pitchers, run on catcher Manny Sanguillen. The thirty-one-year-old Panamanian had batted .328 in 1975, which largely explains why he was the starting catcher. His arm was still strong, but his motion was not ideally quick and compact; his throws were sometimes erratic.

Yet the catcher was only a secondary target. The Reds could run on Sanguillen, but only if they learned to read the pitchers; that, along with the hard-won clues in Morgan's mental files, was the essence of his lesson.

The time has come to put this message to the test. Joe, the potential tying run, is on base for the first time. He continues to concentrate on the pitcher's mannerisms, beating the pick-off attempts with relative ease as his lead grows to a monstrous fourteen feet.

And then he is off! Manny's throw is slightly off the mark, but that is unimportant. Joe has stolen on the key motions of Reuss. And on the very next pitch he steals third. Reuss is visibly upset. Sanguillen is beside himself. Pittsburgh was still ahead 2–1 in the very first game; but, as their agitation revealed, they knew that a crucial skirmish had been lost and that the outcome augured a very long three games for the Pirates.

Unsettled, the leader of the Pirates staff walks Johnny Bench, the hitter who had waited patiently at the plate while the Reuss-Morgan duel ran its course. Perez then singles home Morgan to tie the game, and Griffey doubles home two more runs to excuse the frustrated Reuss after just 2 2/3 innings. Joe ends the day with three steals, the Reds with an 8–3 win.

Joe Morgan's seminar in terrorism on the bases had made its point. The professor had shown the way. The second game's box score showed steals by Foster, Concepcion (2), and Griffey (3), as well as one more for the teacher. The score was 6–1, and the Pirates knew exactly what had hit them: 7 steals in 7 attempts.

Joe Morgan's baserunning technique began with an extraordinary lead off first. TOP: Morgan dives back safely, beating the pickoff throw to Carl Yastrzemski. (Courtesy *Cincinnati Enquirer*) BOTTOM: Alert to the pitcher's moves, Morgan takes off. (Courtesy Cincinnati Reds)

Game two was a 6–1 winner for Freddie Norman; then the teams moved to Pittsburgh for a ten-inning thriller that easily could have turned the series around. Rookie John Candelaria did his best, striking out fourteen Reds. But the outcome, once again, seemed to flow from speed and aggressive baserunning.

Pete Rose had been trying to persuade Ken Griffey to bunt on Candelaria. He hadn't tried, and neither had he got on base. It was now the tenth inning. Candelaria has gone, but the snapping curves of Hernandez in relief seem as formidable as Candy's fastball. Griffey is down to his last strike when, surprising everyone save maybe Pete, he lays one down in front of the plate. Manny picks it up and tries for the tag. Misses.

Now Hernandez, intimidated by Griffey's steals the day before and distracted by his active lead off first, commits a balk. From second, Griffey scores on a ground out and a sacrifice fly.

It is true that speed was not everything. The Reds, in this series, distinguished themselves with the glove, Bench making several outstanding moves in front of the plate and Geronimo getting to fly balls that were outside Al Oliver's range. One spectacular play by Don Gullett (who continued his timely ways with the bat) showed that strength up the middle can also include the skills of a versatile pitcher.

Hitting was timely; pitching was more than adequate. Yet when one looks for the critical difference between the two teams, it is hard to argue with *The Sporting News* headline "Morgan's Marauding Reds Run Over Pirates." Not coincidentally, that page of the October 18, 1975, paper had for its other headline "Morgan Cited as Top Man in Baseball."

The marauding did not stop with the LCS, albeit the Reds' runners stole eleven bases in eleven attempts against the Pirates. Their esteem for Fisk was somewhat higher, but the Reds' rabbits thought they might be able to run off the Sox pitchers, except for the wily Tiant with his near-balk motion.

The Reds applied their now-famous pressure. Sparky pointedly questioned the umpires about Tiant's move, leading to a balk call in the first game. Fisk threw out the first two larcenous Reds, but they persisted and swiped on nine succeeding attempts. Yet, in all candor, it was not speed and intimidation that won this most celebrated of all recent Series. It was resilience. It was the ability to come back and keep coming back, and finally to have a bullpen that could hold. In these attributes Cincinnati was just a little bit richer than Boston (Hertzel, pp. 155–81; Rathgeber, pp. 146–47; TSN).

As the sixth game of the 1975 Series followed its caroming course inside intimate, eccentric Fenway, Pete turned to Pudge and said, "Ain't this one helluva game!" One wonders if anything similar ever happened in October in the House That Ruth Built, that vast plain marked by monuments in center field to the likens of Huggins and McCarthy, Ruth and Gehrig, surrounded by 57,000 seats and the serrated ornamentation of a gargantuan birthday cake.

ROBINSON: "Everyone gets a kick out of beating the Yankees. It was always my favorite win."

PETE: "The New York Yankees have a tradition of World Series dominance."

BENCH: "In New York the media exaggerate everything. They belittle anything that's not the Apple. Thus it was a prideful thing for Cincinnati to beat New York."

KLU: "When Mac [Roy McMillan] went to play for the Mets toward the end of his career, you'da thought they'd just discovered a rookie sensation. Those years of greatness for the Reds, they didn't happen in New York. They didn't happen."

Yankee Stadium: the stage for the broken aspiration of contenders. The Pinstripers are the Lords of October.

Cincinnati fans had tested these generalizations in the past and found them hard and bitter. In 1939, when the Reds and the nation were emerging from a prolonged slump and a prolonged Depression, powerful New York had put them in their place in four straight games. The low point in Redland's long memories came when their redoubtable catcher, Ernie Lombardi, kneed and flattened by the charging "King Kong" Keller, lay dazed on top of the ball while the decisive runs scampered across an unguarded plate.

In 1961 the Reds of Robinson and Pinson, Joey Jay and Jim O'Toole played smartly and lost a tight opener 2–0 to Whitey Ford, then took advantage of New York nonchalance in the second game to win 6–2 and return to Crosley Field even up and looking even better. There, however, the Yankees and Roger Maris hit their stride, winning three straight— the final game by the score of 13–5, four games to one and going away.

To the staid Queen City fans of the 1970s, New York meant more than baseball prowess. It meant violence and disorder. Bob Howsam vividly recalled the final game of the 1973 playoffs against the Mets. "In the seventh inning, when they opened those gates in the outfield, a mob entered. In spite of security officers, they mixed in with our people. They spit on them, tore their clothes. Senator Robert Taft was with us, and we had to wait until the crowd had almost gone, then we left through the dugout and the clubhouse to get to our buses. Even then we had to listen to threats and obscenities."

For all manner of reasons, the emotional stakes were stacked to the limit. And, as is often the case in such situations, the actual deeds did not equal in drama their cathartic potential. In retrospect, say many of the Reds of that era, beating the Yanks was not as impressive as beating the Phils. Then, what Series could match the tensions and reverberations of the previous fall's thriller in Fenway! Perhaps the happiest member of the Cincinnati organization was Big Klu, because "the bop was back." The bats of the sluggers made the decisive points.

If there was a single turning point, it came in the last of the ninth inning of the second and only close game of the four. It was a game in which the Reds' rabbits had been unusually invisible, stealing two bases and suffering one frustrated steal in the midst of their only rally. Aside from a three-run outburst in the second inning, Catfish Hunter, twice victor over the Reds in the Oakland Series, was keeping the bats quiet, especially with runners on base. New York, meanwhile, had tied the game at three all. It looked as though the Catfish might escape the Cincinnati net once again.

Last of the ninth. Two routine outs followed by a grounder to short. Stanley, aware of Griffey's speed down the line, makes a hasty throw aimed at sending the game into overtime. Instead it reaches the dugout, and Griffey reaches second. Morgan, inevitably, receives the intentional walk, bringing up Big Doggie. Griffey: "It seems that every time I am on second base and Perez is at bat that it is automatic he drives me in." Sparky: "Tony likes to end things. That's why we call him Dog. He's tough with the winning run on base." Perez: "I thought that Hunter would try to get ahead of me with a fastball, and he threw one right over the plate." The result was a sharp single through the left side of the infield, sending the flying Griffey home well ahead of Roy White's throw. Cincinnati's RBI leader had driven in one of his biggest (TSN).

Four-three Reds in the game; 2–0 in the Series; on to the dreaded Bronx.

The third game, like the first, was won by a comfortable four-run margin, bringing up the chance for a sweep. In the fourth game the Yankees showed a few things they had not shown before. Mickey Rivers, up to this point stymied by a defense that featured third baseman Rose looking down his collar, finally got a hit and promptly stole second: the first theft off Bench in twenty-six postseason games. Munson, who ended the Series with six consecutive hits, drove Rivers home. But there was little suspense.

Instead there was vindication, not only for a city that had too often played second fiddle, but particularly for a player who had experienced a dismal, untypical summer. Johnny Bench, bothered by injuries, had seen his average sink to .234 with a corresponding drop in home runs (16) und runs batted in (74). It was time.

The Yankees had scored first, giving Ed Figueroa a lead he carried into the fourth, when a two-out single by Foster scored Morgan, who had (guess what?) walked and stolen second. Bench looked at a slider and sent it screaming over Roy White's glove. Fair or foul? Directly into the foul pole. Fair ball. A three-run inning. The Reds ahead.

Now it was the ninth, and the lead had shrunk to 3–2. Figueroa walked the first two batters. With Bench up, Tidrow, who earlier in the Series had got Bench on a double play, was summoned to face the Reds' catcher. This time Bench hit the leftfield seats, putting the ball, the game, and the Series out of reach.

BENCH: "The guys on the team took up the slack for me most of the year. Now I've given something back to them."

For these efforts Bench was voted the Series Most Valuable Player. His team became the first in the National League to win back-to-back World Championships in over sixty years. The city savored a revenge that had been a very long time coming.

When it came to making that elusive summary of the Reds' skills, it was Joe Morgan, author of so many words, who probably chose the best ones. When he spoke to the press, he sounded a little like the people who speak about a city that is too far north to be southern, too far south to be northern, big enough to have all the metropolitan amenities yet small enough to avoid the problems. He said: "The Reds are not a home run-hitting club, nor are we a base-stealing club. We do whatever is necessary to win" (TSN).

Chapter Six.....
AFTER THE BALL

KLU: "There are no heroes anymore. In my day we were all heroes. The fan knows that he is just as good as you except for one thing: you can swing the bat. And as long as you weren't paid enormous sums of money, he didn't resent you at all. The old parks, too, were friendlier. Out at old Crosley Field is where I made most of my friends. The new parks are more efficient, more businesslike; but at Riverfront, for example, you literally cannot hear what is said in the stands. I mean you have to step out of the dugout even to hear the public-address announcement.

"And the press is crucial. Hell in my day you could get in a barroom fight, or get hauled to the jail for being drunk in public, and the manager would have to come down and bail you out, and no one would ever know about it. Why would the press report it? Hell we were all on the same side.

"Nowadays the press is afraid not to report the least little thing. They are afraid someone else will write it up, and then they'll be in trouble. They assume that the fan resents the ballplayers' enormous salaries and wants to read something that will cut these players back down to size. Maybe the press is right in sensing public opinion. The fan still thinks the ballplayer is not all that much better than he is, and maybe he does look for these negative stories. And he sure gets them.

"That's why I say there are no heroes anymore."

Tom Boswell, reporting from Florida, interviews the Mazotas brothers: all in their seventies, residents of Hartford who come south each spring to play some golf and catch a few exhibition games. Though they disagree on many points, each has his reservations about baseball's new economics. One complained about the players' strike, protesting that the inflated salaries were coming out of the fans' pockets. " 'The fans are the suckers. . . . I guess I shouldn't say that, since I'm still one.' " Another brother points out that all the new income generated by TV contracts justifies higher salaries for the players. More power to the players if they can get some of it, but " 'I just hope it doesn't kill the game' " (Boswell, *Time*, p. 251).

If the Mazotases represent a generation of baseball fans in southern New England, perhaps a similar role can be assigned to David Ecker and Warren Hinsch, successful and exceptionally popular Cincinnatians who are now in their sixties. In high school the two formed the heart of teams in all major sports, sometimes to the detriment of their classroom performance. "Tots" Hinsch summarizes: "Sports weren't important to us in those days; they were everything."

As adults, neither remained indifferent to sports. Peg Ecker, David's wife, will proudly tell you that their youngest son is called Buzzie because that was as close as he could come, as an infant, to pronouncing *Kluzewski*. Nor was it an accident that the oldest son's bachelor party took place in a field box at Riverfront. One thing Dave does not see in contemporary professional sports, however, is the kind of effort he himself recalls committing. "After the war [World War II], I went back to Denison and played football for the young Woody Hayes. Now you can say a lot of things about Woody, and I don't want to get into that; but one thing he taught us was that we had no idea of our capabilities. He put me through a program of off-season exercises and drills. They weren't easy. But after a while Woody had me performing at a level I had never thought possible."

Tots, who probably doesn't know how to do anything without enthusiasm, transferred his energies from playing to watching with his characteristic verve. He can still tell you nearly everything about professional sports, including George Foster's batting average before and after he accepted a multiyear contract. When the Bengals came to town, Tots joined with two friends to corner the market on fifty-yard-line seats in the sun. "That's right. Seven Sundays in the fall, surrounded by our best friends. Maybe a little tailgating before or a supper afterwards. This was to be a fixture of our social activity for as long as we lived.

"And those seats! We had our first checks in before they even had the furniture in place in the Bengal offices. Hell we had better seats than the owners!"

Yet a cloud came between the autumn sun and those carefully planned Sunday outings. Ecker: "Just don't let Tots get started on professional sports. He's just as much against them now as he used to be devoted." Marge, Tots's wife, who came to enjoy those football Sundays more than she ever expected, thinks her husband may be cutting off his nose to spite his face. Hinsch: "It was the players' strike that did it. It showed me that they were just selfish; they only cared for the buck and, as for the owners, they weren't one bit better.

"I can sum up how I feel by telling about a time when I was sitting in [Reuven] Katz's office. It was about the time of the first players' strike and [John] Bench was there, grousing about this and that. Now at that time it was true they didn't have a good pension plan. The NFL did, and I happen to know the guy that set that up. They needed something better, but they were asking for the moon. I finally turned to Bench and said, 'You guys want a helluva lot out of your avocation.' Bench looks at me. 'Hell, by your own definition the major-league career lasts only three or four years, whatever it is. Most guys are through at about thirty and ready to start their careers. You've got one of the best tax lawyers, you'll set up trusts and all that, and then you'll want another retirement plan out of your real career!'

"Bench says, 'What's this guy talkin' about?' and Katz says, 'You better listen; he's got a point.'

"Here are these guys on million-dollar, long-term, no-cut deals that take them out of competition. Then they want luxury for life. They haven't even begun their real lives, and already they want the world and ass."

So Tots abandoned his Bengal Sabbath. He also gave up attending, watching, or listening to any professional sporting event. Ecker: "No, I'm not surprised at Tots, although it's always fun to hear him fume and sputter. But I had come to the same position about three or four years before he did. You know, we didn't go in on that great fifty-yard-line club. It seemed like a lot of time, and I had slipped into what you might call a mode of indifference or something. Oh, I'll still go to a ballgame now and then and enjoy it; but I can't get myself to care very much." Consciously or not, Ecker is comparing the level of performance Woody Hayes got out of his amateurs with what he sees on the professional diamond or gridiron.

The defection of these midwestern bellwethers is in marked contrast with the small sample from Hartford. The Mazotases complain about the five dollars for exhibition tickets. They recall as vastly superior the talents of the older generations, monumentally underpaid by today's standards. Yet they still journey to the Fenway and the Bronx for their quota of games; they still make their spring pilgrimage to the Yankee camp; and they still follow both teams on local television. When Boswell asks the Mazotases how often they expect to be in the ballpark during the coming season, the reply comes: " 'In a sense, every day.' "

Luke Appling, the old Chicago White Sox shortstop who vaulted back into the public fancy by hitting a home run in an old-timers' game at the age of seventy-five, discoursed for Boswell on the changing game: "I loved playing . . . Shoot, these [modern] guys don't have fun. They worry." Appling recalls spending many of his Chicago nights speaking before civic groups for nothing but the "ham and peas." "Now they want five hundred dollars to cross the street. They're crazy about money. The players even get paid to give autographs now." As he speculates on the salary that would be commanded today by a shortstop who hit .388 (Appling's mark in '36), Appling mourns the passing of the feeling of warmth and close personal relationships that once existed between the players and the fans. Luke could just as well be Klu, talking about his old pals at friendly Crosley (Boswell, *Time*, pp. 258–59).

The day the dam broke, in terms of flooding professional baseball with money, was New Year's Eve of 1974, when George Steinbrenner announced the signing of Catfish Hunter for $3.5 million. Declared a free agent by arbitrator Peter Seitz, Hunter was released from his obligations to the Oakland As and sold to the winner of what Bowie Kuhn calls the "great Ahoskie fishing contest," after the North Carolina home of the Catfish. The salary offered Hunter compares with the $10 million Steinbrenner had paid for the entire New York franchise. Kuhn identifies Steinbrenner as the player's best friend, citing the several lavish offers (including three that eventually attracted alumni of the Big Red Machine: Gullett, Eastwick, and Griffey) which drew the other owners along in his wake (Kuhn, pp. 169–89).

According to the commissioner's figures, the average ballplayer's salary rose from $52,300 in 1976 to $431,000 in 1986, the greatest percentage rise (53 percent) occurring between 1976 and 1977—the worst possible moment for the talent-rich Reds. Team payrolls, during the same era rose from $31,380,000 to $268,944,000. It is possible to argue about the cause and effect of this increment; it is not possible to dispute its suddenness or its magnitude.

Reuven Katz, a lawyer who represents baseball players, points out that ballplayers' salaries are still not high when compared to those of others in the entertainment business. "The owners overreacted. No question. They spent much more than they needed to, and the fan was totally unprepared to see the ballplayers taking in this kind of money.

"And let's not forget how bad things were for the players, and for how long. The player had two choices: sign or hold out, and holding out was often not much of a weapon. Waite Hoyt, great as he was, tried to get a bit more money from the Yankees by withholding his services. They told him, 'Go ahead. Pick peaches this summer if you want.' "

In the long view, players may have at last been getting economic jus-

Two stages in the economics of baseball are illustrated here. TOP: *Left to right*, Burger Beer's J. F. Koons (father of the Jack Koons interviewed), celebrated announcer Waite Hoyt, and radio network executive Kenneth Church. (Courtesy *Cincinnati Enquirer*) BOTTOM: Representing the age of the agent is lawyer Reuven Katz, *far right*, with his clients, *from left*, Johnny Bench, Pete Rose, and Tony Perez. (Courtesy Reuven Katz)

tice. Yet it was very difficult to understand how this justice was being meted out. It was bad enough to calculate that Dave Winfield, for every three times he came to bat, would be earning as much as Cobb did for a whole season, or as Walter Johnson sought after one of his banner years. It is even worse to realize how much is being lavished on players whose names may not be remembered beyond a single season. The Yankees made some headlines paying Joe DiMaggio the unprecedented sum of $100,000 for a single season. Recently they re-signed a pitcher named Al Holland for $450,000. This was a player that had been cut the year before, who was not even assured a place in the bullpen. This, and other inexplicable inequities, made columnist Shirley Povich throw up his hands at the "checks and imbalances" of modern salaries. Bill Veeck put the question in perspective in his own salty way. The salaries of stars didn't bother him, he said; the problem was "the high price of mediocrity."

The money may be at the root of the problem, but it is not, as Johnny Bench points out, the whole problem: "Something's happened to baseball, to the fans. The Mid-American—whether in Oklahoma or Ohio—is a guy who gets in the pickup and puts the kids alongside him and drives into the city to see a ballgame. He wants his son to see a big-league player because he is something special. He plays a game the way it should be played, but he is also something more than that.

"Now we have sort of taken that away. We've robbed the game of its glamour. Now you just say that if you could become a big-league player, you'd make a lot of money. It used to be more than that.

"Now for the Mid-American, baseball is not the kind of release or escape that he can accept. He is tired of complaining about the high salaries, and he's tired of wondering who's on drugs and who isn't. This is a difficult subject, because when I came up drugs were legal; they were part of the trainer's kit, and you'd be offered these drugs and even have some urged on you and they didn't seem to hurt, so you'd try others under the impression that they'd enhance your performance. And one thing led to another, and now there are different parameters.

"Well, in Middle America this won't do. Mid-America is the crux of us all, the most important part of the country. And these are church-going, God-fearing people who won't accept any of this. Drugs just won't do. And so now baseball has been tainted by the high salaries and the drugs. And going to ballgames just isn't quite so necessary anymore."

HINSCH: "Some guy asked me the other day how I would like it if I had to take a urine test in order to get my CLU license renewed. What do I care? I suppose maybe they ought to give tests to the drivers of those big rigs and others. But hey, if they want to stop use of drugs in sports, it's easy. Regular tests. Test positive once and you're out."

KLU: "The modern player may be less willing to play when injured. Most of us were willing to play any day we could, but then we were only risking our $20,000 salaries. That's a lot different from four million."

John Bench was in the midst of a multiyear contract when he decided to hang it up. Had he played one more year he would have made more money, according to counselor Katz, than in the prior four years combined. Bench defends his decision: "When older players keep on after their prime it is unfair to the fans, to the younger players, and—I guess you could say—to the game. Oh, we still have some of the skills. I can still swing the bat, for example, and as long as I played I still had days that were as good as any I ever had. You tend to focus on those and forget how many subpar days there were between the good ones. That's really not right. Yet the guys keep on. As long as the money's there, they keep on suiting up."

CONCEPCION: "Me and Johnny stay here while most of the players go 'way. Then Pete come back and Tony come back; but it's not the same. Oh the friendship, the personal feelings, they are still there. But Tony is not hitting those home runs when we need them. Pete is not making two-base hit out of one-base hit. We are all older. It is kind of sad."

BENCH: "Yes, the fans are disappointed, and rightly so. But things aren't all that easy for the players either. These days the player has to have an agent, and it is directly in the agent's interest to sell him for as much and as long as he can. The agent begins by working on the player. He tells him how good he is, reminds him of all the bright moments. Then they go into the bargaining, and the management has a whole list of ways in which the player has been a disappointment. Who's he going to believe? And of course meanwhile the press is sniping at him from a bunch of different angles. Sometimes it is hard to know who you are."

KENNEDY: "You want to know what I think is wrong with sport today, just look at this morning's paper. Here is a college athlete who's *offended* by a professional offer, guaranteed no-cut, $350,000. He's OFFENDED! He has never played one minute of professional sport, and they are willing to offer him a guaranteed contract and he's offended."

HINSCH: "You want to know if I never see professional athletes doing their best, and I have to tell you that I don't watch them at all. But from what I read, and from what I recall, I get the very clear notion that they do a lot better in the last year of a contract or when they are about to enter into the free-agent market.

"Once they get their multiyear deals, then forget it. Look at Foster.

He left here for what, one million four? And what did he hit for them, .240, .250?" (Actually, .247 with thirteen homers and seventy RBIs.)

Bowie Kuhn concurs: "By 1980, 42 percent of our players had long-term contracts," a direct consequence of free agency. "I am afraid performance on the field has suffered. While there would always be many players like Pete Rose, Dave Winfield, and Gary Carter who would never give less than their best, too many others have not measured up. This goes to the very heart of baseball's integrity" (p. 171).

KATZ: "They have multiple-year contracts in other sports, but I think they are always subject to review on a year-by-year basis. And that is more reasonable.

"Athletes have all kinds of motivations: they play out of pride, sometimes they play for retribution, to prove something special. They have personal goals. But economic motivation is one of the strong motivations, generally speaking. There is no doubt about that.

"And then you look at the game of baseball. They say it is a game of inches, and it is. Plays are decided by fractions of seconds, balls are caught or deflected sometimes by infinitesimal intervals of distance and timing. To do your very best in a game like this, you need all the motivations that are available. Otherwise you may fall a fraction short."

Disillusion, it appears, arises not so much from high salaries per se as from drug abuse and the multiple-year, guaranteed contract that tempts the player beyond his prime, disinclines him to play when even marginally unfit, and may rob him of economic motivation until the contract's final year. On the other hand, many anticipated problems did not materialize.

The principal surprise is that free agentry has not resulted in the richest teams with the richest markets buying all the top players and running up the pennants, year after year. Steinbrenner's bankroll has come no closer to buying a champion than did Tom Yawkey's in the days of the reserve clause. One is reminded of the legendary newly rich owner who called in the manager and asked what it would take to win the pennant. "We need a top shortstop." "Like who?" "Well I guess Billy Jurges of the Cubs is about as good as there is these days." Owner to owner: "Mr. Wrigley, I'll give you a million dollars for Billy Jurges." Wrigley: "Mr. Smith, I already have a million dollars."

KATZ: "We've seen that you can take a big bankroll and fill some holes on a team. But we haven't ever seen that you could start from scratch and *buy* a team."

What has happened, for reasons that have not been fully explained, is that the championships have been more evenly distributed than ever before. Since 1978, no National League team has repeated as division champion, and every team in the league has finished first at least once. In the American League, the pennant has been won by a different team each year since 1981: seven different teams. What stops the retrospective rotation is a second flag won not by the Yankees or the White Sox or the Angels (to cite the biggest markets), but by the franchise in the league's smallest market, Kansas City: winner in 1980 and '85.

If the fan has been a sucker, as some fans feel, then he has not been taken for as much as he might think. Over the period when salaries were escalating eight- or ninefold, the price of a ticket increased only two- or at most threefold on average. It may be that the age of the free agent has produced a new kind of fan, but at least there are plenty of them. Attendance, overall, has risen every year, on average, and the fantastic (three million for one season in one ballpark) has been achieved more than once.

The opening of the market for player talent could hardly have hit Cincinnati at a less propitious time. The joy of victory did not conceal from management the task at hand: keeping a team whose nucleus consisted of the best players in the game. It would be impossible in this new era— improbable perhaps even under the old conditions—to hold onto them all. So goes the conventional wisdom. Thus, increasingly crestfallen, the Rhineland watched as the Big Red Machine came apart: accidentally and deliberately.

In the off-season following their second consecutive World Championship, they traded Big Doggie along with Will McEnany. Gullett "defected" to a fat Yankee asylum. Twenty-three games into the next season, Rawley Eastwick went the same way, only via St. Louis. (Sparky's last season was '78.) After '79, Joe Morgan went back to Texas. And so ended the 1970s, the Red decade. After '76 they won the division only once, losing in three straight games to the '79 Pirates, a team they had wiped out three times earlier in the decade.

The calendar turned. The seventies became the eighties; George Foster and Ken Griffey departed after the '81 season. Nineteen eighty-three was the last year for Dan Driessen and for Johnny Bench.

PETE: "Looking back at the earlier eighties, the Cincinnati teams seemed to lose their will to win."

The fan has a right to be bewildered by baseball's "new era," a time of unprecedentedly high salaries, outspoken press agents, and questions as to whether "professionalism" still means giving your best effort or now means getting the top buck. Players, moreover, sometimes appear to be more entrepreneurs than simple strong men. They endorse products, they acquire food-and-beverage franchises, they ask for deferred income, and they may eventually acquire a stable of accountants, lawyers, and personal representatives. Some of them, as Luke Appling complains, won't even sign a baseball for nothing. A more important question: What does this kind of individual entrepreneurship do to the game that represents the most delicate of all balances between the single person and the group?

The decline of the Cincinnati hegemony of the 1970s coincided with the rise of baseball's new era to intensify the national experience as seen through Red-colored glasses. This viewpoint—perhaps because of the double exposure—is rich in the wisdom of how to maintain or recapture the best of baseball.

KLU: "The answer is supply. We always knew that there was a gang of talented guys in the farm system waiting for a chance. If someone thought you weren't doing your best, you were gone! Why I've seen a pitcher fail to cover first on a grounder, and the next day he'd be back in the minors.

"But can you do that to a player that has a four-year $2 million contract? And maybe, with the larger number of big-league teams, it is harder to maintain a level of supply. But to me that's the only way: supply. I haven't seen any other.

"It begins with a productive scouting network and a well-run set of minor-league franchises. You recruit the type of player that suits you. You teach him to play ball the way your system indicates. And you send up a stream of trained, talented players ready for big-league testing."

BENCH: "To get back the special quality of baseball, you have to find players who do well on the field but who also present themselves well off the field and in the community."

SPARKY: "You've no idea how hard it is to be a star: to perform well and to live with constant attention focused on you. I was very fortunate at Cincinnati because the key players knew how to do that . . . "

HOWSAM: "Baseball is too great to be ruined by anyone or by any group. But to keep the game great, you have to have players who feel responsible to the fans. Players should get top salaries, but they should also give full effort at all times on the field. They must stay away from drugs, and they should take the time to be friendly with the fans—especially the younger fans, but really all fans—and sign autographs and be available."

KATZ: "You know, even in this day and age there is more to baseball than just money. The free agents don't always make their choices on the top dollar. For example, when Pete finally did leave Cincinnati and we had narrowed down the acceptable choices to four teams, Pete finally took the one that offered the *least* money. Why? Well yes, he liked some of the players, but mostly because it was the kind of team he wanted to play on.

"Let me tell you another chapter in that negotiation that might surprise a lot of people. Among the teams interested in Pete was the Cardinals, and the interest was mutual. But the question was where Pete would play. There seemed to be only one spot, and that was left field. That was where Lou Brock had been starting, and he was still chasing after the 3,000-hit mark. Pete said he didn't want to get in Brock's way as he pursued this goal. St. Louis said, 'That's our problem'; but Pete didn't think that way, and this ended the discussion.

"Johnny Bench is another case in point. He stayed here for years, grossly underpaid, but never making any big issue because he just didn't want to leave. Believe me, he could have made a lot more elsewhere. And I'm sure this doesn't apply just to a few players. I don't know about many of them, but I bet if you knew something about Carl Yastrzemski you'd find the same thing—that he passed up lots of bucks to stay in Boston.

"So even in the meat market that free agentry was supposed to be, it is a lot more complicated than a simple auction with the player routinely picking the highest bidder."

Sunday, August 17, 1986, Cincinnati hosted the San Diego Padres before 27,175 fans who came out to see a couple of teams that weren't heading anywhere important. This crowd may, nonetheless, have witnessed a record-setting event. The starting pitcher, Chris Welsh, the third base-man, Buddy Bell, the shortstop, Barry Larkin, the second baseman, Ron Oester, and the rightfielder, Dave Parker, had all grown up in the Queen City, attended Cincinnati schools, and learned their baseball within a ten-mile radius of Riverfront Stadium. The left side of the infield had actually gone to the same high school (Moeller), although not at the same time. Futhermore, the manager, Pete Rose, inserted himself as a pinch-hitter late in the game, thus adding a sixth to the five hometown boys who had started the game. Unfortunately for the sake of the record books, Pete Rose had given up playing first base regularly by the time Larkin was brought up from the minors; thus the team barely missed having a completely homegrown infield.

The results of the game were not very impressive in spite of home runs by three of the locals (Bell, Oester, and Larkin); but the real question is, what were they all doing there?

WELSH: "Of course I grew up here following the Reds. I was doing well enough as a high school pitcher (St. Xavier) that I was invited down to pitch batting practice. I had a little mustache of which I was proud, and they told me I'd have to cut it off. Yes, just to pitch batting practice for one day. Well of course I did.

"When the Reds were in the Series with the Red Sox, I was a student in Tampa. A couple of us Cincinnati fans got in the car and drove day and night, straight through to Boston. And we didn't even have tickets! We were just hoping to get in somehow. Now how's that for loyalty?

"So when my arm started coming around and I was looking for a place to pitch this year, I naturally called Pete. We're both from the city; we knew each other; I knew he'd give me a chance. I can't imagine anything better for me than catching on here, with Pete, the Reds, and this city."

Barry Larkin, the newest homegrown Red, comes on a lot different from Chris Welsh: "Now, let's get this straight. I didn't grow up here listening to all the Reds games and following their every move and all that stuff. I was no great Reds fan. I am playing for them because they drafted me in the second round out of high school, and then again when I was finishing college [Michigan, three years]. Out of high school, though, I was more heavily recruited for football.

"Oh I like playing here. I get a lot of noise behind me when I step up to the plate at Riverfront; but that's not because I'm a hometown boy. It's because I'm new. Fans like novelty.

"What I'm mainly interested in is playing starting shortstop for some big-league team. If it is Cincinnati, good. If not, OK. I am fortunate enough to have this talent, and I want to use it."

The conversation began to change when I reported the clubhouse gossip that Larkin was playing "smarter baseball" than his equally talented and promising rival. "Where did you learn smart baseball?"

LARKIN: "My father taught me the game. Then I had good instruction at Moeller, and coaches in the summer baseball leagues helped me a lot; plus good coaching at Ann Arbor.

"I have decided that at some time during my career I'd like to play for Cincinnati. I don't live there now; I am in the process of establishing residence in Tampa. But I would like to play for Cincinnati because of family and friends."

Ron Oester was born and reared in Cincinnati, attending the same high school [East/Withrow] as did Ethan Allen, a celebrated native son who came up with the Reds in 1926. Oester was in his teens when Pete Rose came up, playing Oester's eventual position, second base. It is clear that Ron respects his manager, to say the least; Reds-watchers feel Ron is

TOP: Six members of the 1986 Reds had grown up in Cincinnati. *Left to right*, Chris Welsh, Dave Parker, Buddy Bell, Barry Larkin, Ron Oester, and Pete Rose. All played together in only one game: Pete's last. (Courtesy Cincinnati Reds) BOTTOM: The Knot Hole president and the Kid Glove benefit game chairman watch Waite Hoyt, vice chairman of the Powel Crosley Amateur Baseball Fund, autograph baseballs as, *seated*, a young pitcher and Mayor Ruehlmann smile their approval. (Courtesy *Cincinnati Enquirer*)

much like the young Pete in his strong work ethic, his hustle, his determination and his willingness to play when hurt.

OESTER: "This is a fantastic baseball town in all ways. They had me playing organized ball from the age of five, and I've been playing ever since. I surely remember the high school rivalry between Withrow and Pete's old school, Western Hills. They always had a solid team.

"The Reds drafted me in the ninth round, and I've played only here and in the Reds' farm system. I wouldn't really want to play for anyone else. I love this city.

"No one ever gave me anything; I was always taught that you were expected to work for what you got. And that is as it should be. These fans here can be tough on you when you're down because they seem to expect more of the hometown boys. But when you're up, they will give you even more support.

"I love playing here. I'll never forget my first Opening Day here. That was when the dream came true for me. And Opening Days are special here, and they ought to be. The city has meant a lot to baseball, and that ought to be recognized.

"Cincinnati is one of the smaller big-league cities; I believe Kansas City is smaller. And they don't have the high budgets of some other teams. They just couldn't afford to pay all those superstars of the '75 and '76 teams; they had to break the team up gradually. But I think the club has been fair to its players financially. They've always been fair with me.

"But these *are* hard-working people who follow the team. They don't mind high salaries so long as they feel you're giving it all you've got. And of course you'll never play for Pete unless you are a hard worker. He just won't put up with anything else—and that's as it should be."

July 5, 1987, while in the midst of a nine-game hitting streak (.344), Ron Oester was cut down in a second-base play, suffering what many thought might be a career-ending knee injury. He had surgery the next day and began his rehabilitation as soon as physically possible. Other major-league teams, impressed by Ron's characteristic determination, offered him contracts for 1988. The Reds countered with a minor-league offer, and Ron—in spite of what must have been a severe test of his hometown loyalty—accepted.

Buddy Bell was asked if he was pleased to be traded to his hometown team.

BELL: "Yeah, that's right. I wish it hadn't taken so long; I was gone, in effect, for seventeen years. I was drafted by Cleveland after finishing Moeller High and one year at Miami [Oxford, Ohio] and sent to the rookie league in Sarasota. After I came up with the Indians, we moved our home back and forth between here and Cleveland for a few years."

Q: "What's the difference between Cleveland and Cincinnati?"

BELL: "A lot [laughter]. Cleveland's a lot bigger, and you can't really live in the city. At best you're an hour from the ballpark, whereas here you can live anywhere and still get to Riverfront in fifteen or twenty minutes. Cleveland is a good sports town, more so than here in some ways. But the fans there are more . . . rabid, I guess you'd say. More like New York. Is it a better baseball town if the fans are more rabid? It's not the kind of response that players enjoy, or at least I don't. Too much unnecessary pressure."

Q: "Walter Langsam writes that Cincinnati is conservative politically and morally but is quick to accept change when it can be seen that there is profit in it."

BELL: "Yeah. That's pretty good. Yes. But you see, I never think about this city in those terms. To me this has always just been home. Our family moved here when my father was traded to the Reds in 1953, and this has been home ever since. Things change. Old familiar neighborhoods get built up; but to me they still look familiar.

"You were asking about Opening Day ceremonies. Well, they have a pretty big ceremony in Cleveland. But I only experienced that as a player. Here I remember Opening Days from almost before I could remember. My dad took us all—all seven of us—and what a thrill for a kid!

"Not that I regret anything that has happened to me. We enjoyed a lot of things about living in Texas, for example. A lot of good things about that. But all the same . . .

"You see my main feeling is just of good fortune. How many people can say they are doing exactly what they always wanted to do? Playing baseball was at the center of my life from the beginning. True, I went to a high school that was really famous for football, and I got in an argument with football coach "Fuzzy" Faust about that. See I was playing on a summer "select" baseball team, and the schedule overlapped with football. Fuzzy said I should quit that team and concentrate on football.

"Yes, Fuzzy is famous for being persuasive. But this time he didn't have a chance. It is hard to believe how lucky a few of us can be: getting paid for doing what we always wanted to do."

Q: "Were you impressed by the Reds of the seventies and by the way they were presented?"

BELL: "Those were fantastic teams, all right; but then the Reds had been right on the verge of something ever since those teams in the early sixties my father played on. I can't help being a Reds fan; even when I was an American League player, I was always pulling for the Reds in the Series.

"The Howsam/Wagner look went along with those seventies teams, and maybe it did help them project a team unity. But the dress code and all is not important to playing the game, and the way it is preserved here is really just a kind of superstition."

Q: "They tell me that this team, under Rose, lives up to the hard-working image of the seventies."

BELL: "Ha! You could put that as strong as you want. Pete has always believed in hard work; or, to put it better, Pete has always admired people who have succeeded through hard work. That goes with this city, I suppose, but it certainly goes with Pete. And why shouldn't we work hard? I mean, if you are allowed to make your living doing exactly what you've always wanted?"

Dave Parker was the only player interviewed who *volunteered* parallels between the ball team and the city and who repeatedly used the team as a microcosm for viewing society in general.

Q: "Do you think of Cincinnati fans as representing a hard-working, blue-collar area?"

PARKER: "Well, I lived in a place that was more blue-collar than here. It is not just a question of who works hard. Here people are more straightforward, and nice, honest people. More dedicated. In Pittsburgh people worked hard, but they seemed to resent it. Here people work hard and enjoy it. I am not trying to put anyone down, but this is just the way it has appeared to me. The people around here are just nicer."

Q: "Cincinnati has been called conservative."

PARKER: "Yes. You can see that right here on this ballclub, with its rules against facial hair, the black shoes, the traditional way of wearing the uniform.

"As far as the city goes, that is fair enough. But I want to live in a conservative city. That's why, after I got married, I was so interested in coming back here. It is the kind of place you want to raise a family. There is interest in youth here, the Knot Hole program and so forth. And there is interest in good education: the Seven Hills School, Dougherty, and the like [these are among Cincinnati's best private schools]. And there is a major drug problem out there in society. This city does as good a job as any place—better than most—in dealing with this problem."

Q: "Does being conservative suggest intolerance of 'alternative life-styles,' and of minority views?"

PARKER: "Yes, you can see that right here on the ball team, too. But we are getting somewhere. We now have our red shoes back, along with the privilege of wearing our stirrups a little bit higher. For a long time, though, Cincinnati held the line against change and tried to preserve baseball in what you might call its more primitive form. Not just the dress code, but also the low salaries and the refusal to go into the free-agent market."

Q: "Is that because this is one of the smaller big-league cities?"

PARKER: "I don't think so. Every time I came in here, this ballpark was full. They were makin' money. They were makin' lots of money."

Q: "Did those teams in the mid-seventies represent some kind of turning point?"

PARKER: "I think so. Of course there were other good teams here too, but there is a big difference between comin' into town and saying, 'Hello, I'm Dave Parker playing with the last-place Reds' and being with the first-place Reds. The difference is winning, and when you win you do a lot for a city financially as well as in terms of morale. I saw that happen in Pittsburgh too."

Q: "If the team is moving gradually away from its conservative style, is that true of the city as well?"

PARKER: "What's true of the team is more or less true of the city. I represent one of the so-called minorities here, and things are not exactly what they should be, but they are getting better. Some of these things take time. And in the city I've seen a lot of changes, especially since I came back here. The acceptance of Ken Blackwell [black vice-mayor] is one sign. Another sign is the acceptance of minorities in the school system and in the various neighborhoods throughout the city. So things are coming along."

Q: "In an imperfect world, this place will do?"

PARKER: "Listen, let me tell you something. I have been around this country now for a number of years, and I've been in I think all the major cities, and I tell you I haven't found any place I'd rather live than right here."

People who follow baseball closely have commented on the surprising number of big-leaguers to have come out of Cincinnati's Bently Post American Legion team or from Western Hills High School. There is some question, however, as to whether the Reds have ever taken a keen interest in local talent, having watched not only Dave Parker and Buddy Bell get away but also Jimmy Winn, Kent Tekulve, and others. A feature in a local paper July 27, 1986, showed that thirty-two young athletes from the metropolitan area were under contract to major-league teams. Only three of them (including Larkin) had been claimed by the Reds.

And yet if you listen to the men who grew up in Cincinnati and also play there, you certainly do not get the idea of random selection. Pete Rose, perhaps the prototype for all hometown heroes (see Epilogue), feels that the city and the sport have a unique mutual attraction. The others, some of them, feel they owe their skills to the special sports programs lavished on the local youths. Others recognize that the habits and values that made them successful emerged from family and community. They seem to like the city not just because it supports the ball team, but because of the consistent, conservative matrix that defines both the city and the team. Work hard, play hard. Be patient, Don't get out of line. Do your best, keep your head down, and you'll get what is coming to you.

BENCH: "This whole city is a bunch of semijocks. They are relaxed; they have a good time. I can always get a golf game. Living here and playing for the Reds, it's like being a member of the best social club in town."

SPARKY: "Living and working in Cincinnati is like being part of one big family. Everybody knows you and talks to you, but they don't bother you. They are very supportive."

KATZ: "In the off-season of 1976–77, when the Reds and Pete were so far apart on contract terms, I decided the only solution was to take the issue to the public. Pete did this himself for a while, then, after spring training started, I had to do most of it myself. The result was that Dick Wagner got hundreds, thousands of letters, and they ran about five to one, I gathered, in favor of giving Pete something close to what he thought he should be worth.

"They started out offering just above $200,000. We thought we should get $400,000. Using the people of Cincinnati as a kind of jury, we would have been able—I honestly think—to get our way completely."

KLU: "Of course, most of our friends have something to do with baseball; but not all. And I've never known anyone who has lived in Cincinnati for more than six months who didn't really like it. At first this city looks pretty ordinary. The good things are not flashy and obvious. But once you get to know the place, you wouldn't trade it. Six months living here and your cry if you have to leave!"

Ted Kluzewski proved his point by keeping Cincinnati as his residence even while playing for other teams at the end of his career. So did his teammate Gus Bell, as well as Brooks Lawrence, Leo Cardenas, and Jim O'Toole. More recent Reds who have kept their homes in the city in spite of trades or retirement include Lee May and Eddie Milner (both of whom have just returned to the team), and Ken Griffey. Dave Parker, although traded to Oakland over the winter of 1988, has not moved his residence. (This small sample proves little, but it is worth noting that of these nine players, three are white, one Hispanic, and five black.)

There may be, as Ted Kluzewski says, no more heroes in the age of high salaries. The Mid-American father, according to Johnny Bench, may not find a special reason for wanting his youngsters to see big-league baseball firsthand. There may be no antidote for disillusion.

But if there is one, is it not in the relationship between a team, a sport, and a community? Does playing for a certain team mean more, as Dave Parker suggests, when the team is a symbol for the community? Will playing for Courter Tech, Moeller, Withrow, or Western Hills lead equally to the conclusion that the best place to play baseball is beside the Ohio River? Pete Rose and Reuven Katz, Sparky Anderson and Bob Howsam, Ted Kluzewski and Gene Ruehlmann—all have discovered and built upon a set of special relationships between this sport in this city.

Chapter Seven.....
THE CITY AND THE GAME

If, as Tom Boswell insists, "time begins on Opening Day," then nowhere outside Cincinnati is the event marked so clearly in holiday colors. Offices close at noon. The Findlay Market Association—following a tradition that precedes living memory—organizes a parade with bands and floats, wending its way through the heart of this city, past the cheering throngs at Fountain Square, and on to the now-adjacent ballpark. Even a well-known out-of-town brewery has seen fit to swell the marching order with its trademark coach and Clydesdales.

CONCEPCION: "Opening Day here you find nowhere else."

BELL: "Of course, I remember this day as a kid; but even for the players this is a very exciting moment."

EPR: "Opening Day is a big event, promoted by the Chamber of Commerce and downtown restaurants. Tickets are much in demand, as business professionals like to take their customers and clients. When there was some talk of cutting back on the festivities, the preservation of Opening Day became a cause célèbre."

Dick Bray, a long-time sportscaster from the Crosley era, who introduced "fans in the stands" interviews, insisted that Opening Day in Cincinnati was like New Year's Eve in Times Square and Mardi Gras in New Orleans rolled into one.

Although the regular-season attendance may fall into certain categories, Opening Day is another story. Some schools close, at least in the afternoon; otherwise the student has only to show that he is being taken to the game and he is excused without question and with much envy. The city's prestigious downtown gathering place, the Queen City Club, puts on a special Opening Day buffet that is routinely sold out a year in advance.

There is no question that, by early April, Cincinnati is ready for songs of spring. Winters are invariably damp and sometimes prolonged. North winds sweep down from the Great Lakes and west winds roar up the

TOP: The traditional Opening Day Parade passing Fountain Square on the way to Riverfront Stadium. BOTTOM: An Oktoberfest dance downtown. (Both photos courtesy Greater Cincinnati Convention and Visitors Bureau)

Ohio, scuffing the tops of the fabled seven hills. While looking for green buds and robins, the good burghers are also absorbing the news from the Grapefruit League and following the progress of native sons in major-league training camps from Florida to Arizona.

So when the team comes north, the Queen City is more than ready for cheerful predictions concerning the upcoming season. Opening Day itself may be frosty, but red knees will not deter the baton-twirlers. Nor will visible puffs of breath curtail the speakers representing civic groups come to honor the heroes of the season past, ring in the promising new, and—in general—strike up the band.

The National League has encouraged the notion that, at least on Opening Day, Cincinnati is the center of the baseball world (and as Boswell would say, what other world is worth talking about?). Uniquely, the Reds are always scheduled to open the season at home. This would be normal only in alternate years, and sometimes the Reds have begun along with the pack. When their first series would normally be out of town, however, they have the National League opening day all to themselves, sometimes sharing it with Baltimore (or in other times, Washington), where the president of the United States is expected to throw out the American League's first ball, a custom begun by a Cincinnatian named William Howard Taft.

There are good reasons for singling out the Queen City. Most fans know that professional baseball dates itself from the 1869 Red Stockings, as many also are aware that the city revolutionized the big-league game by introducing night baseball. Moreover, if Harry Ellard can be credited, the groundbreaking Red Stockings led to such innovations as a baseball writer, a reporter who traveled with the team, as well as the custom of publishing ball scores on a daily basis. The city played a crucial role in founding the first league of professional teams in 1876.

When expelled from the National League in 1882, Cincinnati then became an organizational center for the American Association; and, having finished first in that league, the team took on the Chicago White Stockings in the prototype for the World Series. The "father of the World Series," as it is known today, is none other than that prominent Cincinnatian Garry Herrmann. Whether this is a deserved title or not, it is true that Herrmann, as chair of the National Commission, functioned as the commissioner of baseball prior to the establishment of that office. More recently Commissioner A. B. "Happy" Chandler placed his office in Cincinnati, and Warren Giles made his acceptance of the presidency of the National League conditional on operating out of the Queen City.

The last century has witnessed a tendency for all organizations to establish national offices in New York or Washington, baseball included. Cincinnati has furnished, from time to time, an interesting countertrend. Manhattan's Broadway may be the avenue of opening nights, but the ballpark in Redland has been the official and symbolic place where, every spring, baseball time begins to tick.

Throughout America the melting snows and the rising sap have long been associated with the pop of the glove and the crack of the bat. Growing up in the Midwest, a lad would be hard pressed to avoid baseball in one form or another. In Cincinnati steps have been taken to make sure that the baseball virus is implanted deep and early. Much of the credit for this belongs to Powel Crosley, who acquired the Reds in the Depression. Crosley founded the Knot Hole Club, an organization for school children which used a variety of interrelated lures to ensnare the younger generation (see chapter one).

What fatally ensnared the original Knot Hole generation was the rise of the Reds from a pathetic last to pennants in 1939 and 1940 under the leadership of Bill McKechnie. Watching in person on their designated Knot Hole days, the youth learned to imitate the moves of a Billy Werber or a Harry Craft. Play by play, night and day, the radio network mesmerized parents and teachers, girls and boys with exploits of Alex Kampouris and Ival Goodman, Frank McCormick and Ernie Lombardi, Bucky Walters and Johnny Vander Meer.

Equipment was provided to the Knot Hole teams by the city, with an assist from Crosley. Eventually, the Reds inaugurated "Kid Glove Day," an exhibition game whose proceeds provided gloves, bats, and balls for the youngsters of the cities involved. Bill DeWitt, a committed if not a popular owner of the Reds in their latter days at Crosley Field, followed Crosley's example of generosity in the form of gifts to improve baseball facilities in the city's parks and playgrounds. This was done with little fanfare and for little public credit. Cincinnatians were in fact taken off their guard by DeWitt's tearful regret on relinquishing his local baseball connections.

The interaction between the Reds countryside and the ball team is encouraged in order to sell tickets, but it incidentally creates a kind of unity that seems to depend on athletic teams. When the ballplayers visit Columbus, Indianapolis, Lexington, Louisville, and Huntington, they meet not only with chambers of commerce and Rotarians but with student groups as well. Gordy Coleman, the director of the Reds Speakers Bureau, himself visits towns and villages on a regular basis all year long. On at least one "Farm Night" at the ballyard, Johnny Bench allowed himself to be photographed milking a prize cow—something that a big-city boy might hesitate to do. Like athletes in other sports and other cities, many of the Reds players have been generous with their time in support of the young, the handicapped, and social and religious groups of various kinds.

Along with baseball, Cincinnati is proud of its music. Not only does the May Festival flourish, but the city has a summer sesson of *grand* opera, for a long time held on the grounds of the famous zoo, sopranos and tenors competing with lions and exotic birds as the strains of Puccini filled the damp summer air. Sometimes the two loves of the Queen City come together. Johnny Bench did a dramatic reading of "Casey at the Bat" accompanied by the symphony's Pops aggregation. Recently, a poster showed the director of that ensemble, Erich Kunzel, posed back to back with Pete Rose, each holding the baton of his trade. "Kunzel and Hustle" was the motto for promoting a symphony benefit night at Riverfront. Louise Nippert, part-owner of the Reds and a sponsor of the symphony, has a favorite usher at Music Hall, one who will unfailingly apprise her of the score of the ongoing Reds contest.

All year long baseball and community intertwine, from the Winter Reds Caravan of stars and speakers to the summer leagues for youngsters. And Opening Day, as Mayor Ruehlmann says, is the biggest day of the year.

Opening Day in Cincinnati is also a festival. It might be called Aprilfest. There already are Maifest and Oktoberfest, and an annual Riverfest. The archives of the Historical Society are full of photographs of groups perpetuating such German traditions as the turnerfest, saengerfest, and schuetzenfest, some of which continue to the present day.

My wife, who is from a less Germanic part of the Midwest, used to tease me by having me recite, for the benefit of disbelieving friends in Wyoming or Washington, the names of my teammates on the Knot Hole team of my Cincinnati youth: Stricker and Streit; Fibbe, Gauspohl, and Glass; Koons, Hinsch, Ruth, Heimerdinger, and Weitzel. Our counterparts on the other side of town, who usually beat us, were producing eventual major-leaguers named Wehmeier, Rose, Brinkman, and Zimmer.

Baseball was not the invention of German-Americans, but its history has been marked by the people named Ruth and Gehrig, Frisch and Wagner, Heinie Groh and Germany Schaefer. To judge by names alone, the story of Cincinnati and baseball seems overwhelmed by the Germanic: from Herrmann and Bettman, to Howsam and Ruehlmann, to Rose and

One example of the mutual support of team and community was a benefit at Riverfront for the Cincinnati Pops Orchestra. A poster for the event featured conductor Erich Kunzel and Reds manager Pete Rose. (Courtesy Pat Koons)

Oester. "Sparky," I exclaimed to George Anderson during our chat, "you had so much to do with Cincinnati baseball, it's too bad your grandmother wasn't German." "She was! She was!" he chirped in reply and proceeded to tell me her name.

"Vas you effer in Zinzinnati?" This phrase, in the 1930s, was used by one of the local breweries as its slogan. Which brewery? It hardly mattered, since their names were Wiedemann, Schoenling, Hudepohl, and Burger (formerly Windisch-Mulhauser). Beer goes with the festivals, or—it may be more correct to say—the festivals go with the beer. They both relate to baseball.

Just as the German inclination toward festivals surely had a part in making Opening Day the annual ritual it has become, so the local beer industry had a large part in selling baseball—especially via radio and television—to the city and its surrounding region. In the early days of radio broadcasting, the team owners were convinced that live broadcasts would hurt attendance at the ballpark—just the opposite of what turned out to be the case. Because Powel Crosley owned both the team and the leading radio station/network, he was more inclined than other owners to experiment. Broadcasts at first were underwritten by chewing-tobacco, cigarette, and gasoline companies; but the first well-established Reds network was assembled by Burger Beer, through the Midland Advertising Agency, and the knowledgeable commentary of Waite Hoyt. The network superimposed a pattern of beer distribution on the pattern of baseball loyalty: each enforcing the other. Burger sold its beer as far north as Columbus, as far west as Indianapolis and Louisville, as far east as Huntington, West Virginia, and south through Kentucky and into Tennessee.

As to the closeness of the ties, listen to Jack Koons, who, as president of both the ad agency and the brewery, had nurtured the connection between Burger and baseball:

KOONS: "There came a time when I knew I was going to have to sell Burger. Small breweries were under pressure from those with a national market. You could survive, but it was a struggle. There were certain problems I just didn't want to face anymore, including the annual battle with the unions. The buyer was surely going to be another brewery, and I was going to have to find a sure attraction. There was really only one, and that was the baseball broadcast contract. Without baseball, Burger was next to nothing. So I carefully negotiated a long-term contract through Midland with the Reds, and then I had something to sell. The rest was easy." Burger became Hudepohl.

The labor history of the brewing industry has also produced a priceless

The two most celebrated radio voices of the Reds exchange views: Waite Hoyt, *left*, and Red Barber. (Courtesy *Cincinnati Enquirer*)

example of the way social change tends to operate in a city such as Cincinnati. The workers—because their product at some stages requires round-the-clock ministrations—were routinely putting in thirteen- to eighteen-hour days, and sometimes showing up on Saturdays and Sundays as well. Even though other industries had achieved much more humane hours, the owners, arguing special needs, persisted. The workers struck. The owners hired scabs and went on with their business, finally bringing the strikers to their knees. Then—and *only* then—did the owners concede to the workers the shorter hours demanded in the strike! (Downard, chap. 7)

As the names of most American beers indicate, the beverage has a special meaning to German-Americans. G. A. Dobbert, chronicler of the Cincinnati Germans, claims that the beer and the language were all that kept this community together during the anti-German days of World War I. Although it has surely had its cycles of popularity, the overt interest in German roots and customs was abundantly evidenced in the 1983 celebration of the tricentennial anniversary of German immigration. The Over-the-Rhine neighborhood, once the center of the German community, had degenerated into a slum until it was partially restored and added to the roster of historic districts. It is now in the process of gentrification.

In 1985 a feature writer for the *Enquirer* asked "Does Our German Image Still Fit?" The decidedly positive answer was published in the *Sunday Tristate Magazine* of September 8. Kathy Doane found German customs continuing up to the present. Bilingual schools still exist, as do dozens of societies maintained for purposes ranging from the promoting of cooking and singing to the relief of needy citizens of German lineage. Aside from the well-known festivals are lesser ones devoted to soccer and dancing, drinking and shooting.

The persistent preservation of German culture in "Zinzinnati" does not suggest parallels with modern Germany, East or West. Rather, it speaks for links with nineteenth-century Europe and to a kind of transformation that made German-Americans distinguishable both from Germans and from other Americans. Novelist Herman Melville seemed fully aware of this quality as, in *Redburn*, he described those Germans embarking for America on ships tied up at Liverpool. Days before departure, he reports, they came aboard to make everything comfortable, the old and the young, the "laughing girls in bright-buttoned bodices, and astute, middle-aged men with pictured pipes in their mouths." Every evening they would gather on the forecastle to sing and pray. To close your eyes and listen to "their fine ringing anthems," "you would think you were in a cathedral."

And among these . . . Germans my country counts the most orderly and valuable of her foreign population. It is they who have swelled the census of her Northwestern states . . . sowing the wheat of the Rhine on the banks of the Ohio, raise the grain, that, a hundred fold increased, may return to their kinsmen in Europe. (N.Y.: Doubleday, 1957, p. 162)

These lines appeared in a novel Melville first published in 1849, just at the time of the large-scale German migration to the United States. Germans came to places such as southern Ohio, settled more or less permanently, worked hard and efficiently, whether at agriculture, manufacturing, trade, or the professions. While preserving some measure of their Germanness, they set a strong example of loyalty to family, church, and community.

They also liked their beer and song, and they thought Sunday was a good day for both, thus contributing to the lingering fight over the "continental Sabbath" versus the strict Pietistic observance of Sunday as a day fit only for quiet worship. This was the essence of the dispute that got the Red Stockings expelled from the National League (see chapter one). Here was the heritage of "champion sausage-eaters and beer-drinkers" such as Garry Herrmann, who, incidentally, was also justly famous for his creation of a model city utility. Herrmann's memory lingers at Riverfront in a variety of sausages, including the local favorite Hamilton mets, heaped high with sauerkraut, and accompanied by the beer of one's choice, national or local.

PETE: "There are a lot of Germans here who are conservative: beer-drinking and hardworking."

KNIGHT: "No question the people in Cincinnati are eight-to-five people, hardworking, conservative, German background."

These hardworking Cincinnatians with the German names may become wealthy, but not ostentatious. On the other hand, they are not stingy, and they know how to have a good time. And they tend to formalize these good times into festivals and contests, rituals and recurring celebrations. People who observe parts of the Midwest—and perhaps especially Cincinnati—seem to feel that to live there involves breathing this pattern of life along with the very atmosphere. Growing up in Cincinnati, whether your name is O'Brien or Caproni or Schultz, you probably acquire some of these "Germanic" traits.

There is another aspect of the Cincinnati style that may or may not be Germanic but which is surely characteristic and coincides with the city's baseball preeminence. Reduced to a single word, it might be called *professionalism*. You get what you pay for. When you find out you need something, you go out and try to get the best there is. This spirit is in theoretical conflict with voluntarism—corporate or otherwise. In practice, however, the two often work hand in hand.

The city's early attempts to deal with prostitution offer a case in point. When first apprehended, the woman would be given a lecture on the evils of the oldest profession. A second arrest, however, would lead to her registration and a schedule of regular health inspections.

Fighting another kind of fire offers a variation. Confronted with the dangers inherent in leaving conflagrations to the efforts of competing volunteers, the city established, in 1853, the nation's first professional fire department and consistently furnished it with the latest and best equipment.

Professionalism seems often to ally itself with technology. The steam fire engine is one example; so were the recently acquired foam nozzles that saved the flood of 1937 from becoming a floating inferno. So, in a different context did the city's railroad represent the purchase of a piece of outstanding technology to remedy the city's economic problems.

Organized baseball, in the 1860s, was a mixture of amateurs and professionals. It was common knowledge that many teams paid some of their players; perhaps some of them secretly reimbursed an entire team. When certain residents of the Queen City decided that a proud city needed a team they could be proud of, they resorted to neither subterfuge nor hypocrisy. They went out and bought the best they could get; the best, at that time, including only one player from the home town. To describe the legendary 1869 Red Stockings accurately is to say that they were the first *fully and openly* professional baseball team. And were they good!

In the 1960s it became apparent that the baseball team might leave the city, but that a modern stadium not only might keep the Reds, but also might attract a big-league football team. Professional sports were perceived as economically advantageous. In getting the stadium underway—another piece of technology that could sit by the river and resist eighty feet of floodwater, changing its interior shape to adjust from a diamond to a gridiron, while the scoreboard flashed revealing replays and irresistible commercials—voluntarism emerged to help the professionals through some tight places. The plan and the design were the best—or were meant to be the best—that money could buy. So, of course, were the athletes.

The athletes who play for the Reds today attest, over and again, that no one resents their high salaries so long as they work hard, do their evident best, and provide services rendered for services paid. Bob Howsam, on assuming the general managership, won instant approval by asking first to see the operating budget and then requesting significant new funds for scouting and player development. In the same spirit Cincinnati, while by no means alone in developing long-range plans, was the first city to employ a permanent, full-time professional planner. You get what you pay for.

The Big Red Machine (speaking of technology) was a triumph of balance: power and speed; high batting averages and defensive skills; adequate starters and a strong bullpen. Similarly, the city itself is often presented in terms of balance: delicately poised between large and small, North and South, it is said to have the best features of these polarities without suffering their deficiencies. This balance is maintained by avoiding bumps and jolts.

Strikes and angry demonstrations tend to evoke nothing but resistance. The way to achieve social gains is to avoid politicizing the issues. Do it quietly. Naively or not, the brewers were sending the message that concessions would have arrived sooner *without* the strike, just as the authorities were telling the rioters in Avondale that social progress would not emerge from social upheaval.

Q: "Some people feel that the underside of conservatism is lack of social progress, or at least retarded social progress."

EPR: "Well, I can't really comment on that. Maybe that takes a more distant perspective than I have. But I do think that one generation will never be able to remove feelings that have existed for centuries.

"When we looked at the problems of the black community here, they seemed to come under a number of headings. One of them was unemployment. To deal with this we worked with the business community, which formed a Committee of Twenty-eight; there were fourteen black and fourteen white leaders, mostly from the business community. They created, located, and publicized job opportunities for the black community. Another business group raised seed money that could be used to fund programs for housing and recreation.

"In the late sixties, we were hardly starting from scratch. Cincinnati had one of the first successful slum-clearance projects, I think, in Laurel Homes. Cincinnati had one of the first planning offices. The area attracted one of the New Deal 'green towns.'

"In the past, much of the financing came from the federal government, and federal support is still a necessary part of this program. But the initiative comes from our local community: though government, business, and citizen participation.

"Cincinnati also had strong religious leadership, and that was very helpful on certain problems. When I became mayor, I became aware that—for good reason or not—many blacks just did not feel welcome at city hall. So we undertook a program of visiting black communities and churches."

Q: "That is a good idea, but it is not original, is it?"

EPR: "No it was not. Mayor John Lindsay did it as part of his campaign in New York; but there was an important difference. He made it a media event. We did just the opposite, keeping as low a profile as we could. My wife frequently accompanied me, and we didn't ever decide which church we were going to visit until the last moment. So there was no media coverage.

"We found those visits inspirational as we came to understand the aspirations of the black community. In the end their goals were no different from ours. By getting to know the religious leaders and black community leaders, things turned around so that blacks no longer felt out of place in the city offices. There is now a Metropolitan Area Religious Coalition of Churches that includes black churches and makes a substantial political contribution. Surburban churches of all denominations came, in the late sixties, to sponsor and form partnerships with poorer congregations. A lot of good work was done this way.

"Much racial progress in the sixties was due to the leadership of Myron Bush who, as councilman, became an effective spokesman for the black community and was *highly* respected by blacks and whites. He and I were able to work together on a daily basis.

"Also, the Board of Education made some important decisions, including one that allowed parents to send their children to any public school they wanted, regardless of districting."

KNIGHT: "There were hard feelings between the Reds management and some of the black players, but it seemed more to do with personality than race. I never heard people who live here make antiblack remarks."

CONCEPCION: "This is a very friendly city. We don't have to put up with things like we did in some southern towns: Columbus, Georgia, or Charlotte, North Carolina, where we weren't treated so well."

PARKER: "This is a good place to raise a family. There are good schools. On minority questions there has been progress since the days when I was growing up here."

SPARKY: "I never knew any black player to feel uneasy in Cincinnati."

EPR: "While much remains to be done, we have done as well here, I think, as any city our size that has been faced with the problem."

BENCH: "The situation for minorities isn't too bad here. Maybe you don't have too much leeway, and certainly nobody is pushing you up the ladder. But, on the other hand, nobody is trying to brush you aside, either, like I seem to see in a lot of other places.

"There was ferment and protest here, too, in the early seventies, but it never got out of control. There has been progress for minorities, but it doesn't make headlines. You take what you can get, and you sort of settle in. This is a kind of 'settled-in' city."

EPR: "The Reds of the seventies, with the conservative, old-fashioned image, were completely consistent with the city of Cincinnati.

"There is a great, great German heritage here. There are other strong groups here: blacks, Italians, Irish. But it does't really matter what your ancestry was. You can feel this influence.

"It is a conservative community with a strong work ethic. It has not been a high-growth area in recent years, but that is not all bad. We haven't had to deal with a lot of the problems that come with growth and sprawl.

"So Cincinnati has been blessed with stability. The charter form of government has provided us with political stability, supported by a professional city manager. The wide diversity of local commerce and manufacturing has given us some economic stability.

"And this business community has provided the city with corporate citizenship. The importance of this can hardly be overstated. Some political leaders, for example, have confronted the business community and created a situation where politics and business are in opposite corners. Here we have worked openly and cooperatively together, and the corporate volunteers have been enormously important in solving problems ranging from the building of the expressways, making a stadium possible, and getting better minority housing.

"And as I've already mentioned, we have strong religious leadership, and that is very important.

"All of this adds up to the ability to face the problems of the community and to work toward solutions in a low-profile spirit of cooperation. We don't have to call press conferences or have street demonstrations or strikes."

SPARKY: "Cincinnati is a very pleasant city. Not flashy. There are people there who have a lot of money, but you'd never know it. They make it their business not to show their wealth. It's that way with the families who own the Detroit team too.

"But the fans are not alike. In Cincinnati they'll get on you, but their choice of words is restrained. In Detroit they'll throw some juicy ones at you. The four-letters ones and like that. The Reds fans will tell you what they think, all right, but they won't use some of those nastier words.

"Cincinnati is a family-orientated city. They are really nice people, and they do a lot of things in family groups.

"There are about thirty families that more or less run the city. And they all know each other, and they work together pretty well. They will come forward when they're needed. They are community-oriented. It is a place where they put community first. That's what makes it laughable to think they'd ever lose their ball team."

EPR: "Things may be different now, but there was a spirit of cooperation that arose out of the late sixties and prevailed during the early seventies. Let me tell you one story. I want to give you the whole story because it shows the way we sometimes use our favorite sport and how we can work together.

"There is a grade school in the West End, Hayes School, 90 percent black. I had been invited down there to meet the student mayor. They had a black lady principal, Vivian Beaman, whom I admired so much. She had such discipline.

"One of the things she had done was to create a student government modeled on the city's, and she had arranged this visit. I also talked with the school's white assistant principal, who told me a story about a white policeman who came to the school to deliver a summons. The assistant said to him, 'Every time we see you, we know it's bad news. Isn't there something good you can do for us?' 'Like what?' 'Well, one thing might be to coach our Knot Hole team. These kids want to play, and they don't have a manager.' The police officer agreed to coach and got some of his friends to do the same. Now they've got their four teams organized, but they're stuck because they don't have any equipment. So I told the assistant principal, 'OK, I'll see what I can do to take care of that.'

"That same day I was speaking to a fund-raising luncheon of a group of Jewish businessmen, and we discussed various city projects. So I told them about this white policeman and the black Knot Hole teams without any uniforms or equipment. I was told to call the leader of this business group and tell them how much it would take. I did so, and within ten days we had fully outfitted teams of black school kids, equipped through the generosity of the Jewish businessmen and managed by white policemen.

"And you know what happened? Soon we've got a whole rash of teams from the poorer neighborhoods with policemen for coaches, and I am spending my time looking for money!"

The Cincinnati game, athletic and political, might have been called on account of apathy had it not been for the two towering figures introduced in chapter two. Robert Howsam was born into a family of sports promoters, administrators, and stadium builders; his son successfully carries on. Astutely political by nature, Howsam learned his fundamentals at the feet of his father-in-law, Colorado's "Big Ed" Johnson. Responsible for the team, Bob could not help becoming involved with the city.

Gene Ruehlmann, wanting the best for the city, could not help becoming involved with the team and the stadium. His present law office offers a blimp's-eye view of the Third Street Distributor—the highway mixmaster that worked—and, just beyond, of the stadium itself, its bright turf and colorful seats. Looking out his window, Gene is reminded of his own athletic career, which included playing football for a University of Cincinnati team that beat Big Ten rival Indiana. "That was *not* the Indiana team," Gene confesses, "on which Kluzewski played!" In this setting the former mayor is asked to give his own impressions of the city he has served so long and well. Looking toward the diamond barely concealed behind the walls of Riverfront, he replies, "Cincinnati is a jewel."

Robert Howsam, once voted Cincinnati's outstanding ambassador, says, "The ball team must always carry—and carry proudly—the name of the city across the front of the road uniform. At home it doesn't matter. But an athletic team can give positive visibility to a city the way nothing else can—not even a great and famous corporation like Procter & Gamble.

"Being responsible for any enterprise that is so visible is not so easy. Everything can go wrong, from the Zamboni to the ticket-printer. And many days the press will just rip you open, from one end to the other. When these things happened and I got down to the bottom point, I would leave the office and just walk around Riverfront during a ballgame. Seeing all those people there—families, couples, kids, loving the game—somehow that made it all worthwhile."

Epilogue.....

ROSE AT HOME

LARKIN: "Does Rose reflect the city? Hell the city reflects Rose. Pete Rose has Cincinnati following him about anywhere he wants to go."

PARKER: "He reflects what basically this whole area is like—that basically is hard work and dedication. A down-to-earth everyday guy who works extremely hard. That's why he's accepted here. That's the way you achieve in everyday life."

Twenty-four years after Pete Rose signed with the Reds and reported to the Geneva farm club, Charlie Hustle came back to Cincinnati. Fourteen years after he helped dedicate Riverfront Stadium by rounding third and heading for Ray Fosse, Pete was back at the ballpark with a different home. On the door it said "manager."

Pete's homecoming was an attenuated celebration, no part of which was more memorable than the evening of September 11, 1985, when a single off San Diego's Eric Show broke baseball's one apparently unbreakable record. Pete had 4,192 hits; Ty Cobb, 4,191. The event was more nostalgic than germane. The 1985 team was not the Big Red Machine but was struggling toward a second-place finish. In terms of personal history, though, it punctuated a career that set enough precedents to make Rose, according to *The Sporting News*, the Athlete of the 1970s and to assure him a prominent place in Cooperstown.

In the summer of 1987 there was no button-eyed, crouching switch-hitter, following pitches carefully into the catcher's glove or slashing them toward the gap and taking an aggressive turn at first. There was no spiking of the ball at the inning's end, no headfirst slides. There was still, however, a unique, insistent presence: a hard-working, durable professional. Although his role had gradually shifted, Rose remained highly visible: unpolished but undaunted; competitive, goal-oriented, persistent. Were these the qualities the city liked to see in itself? At least they had given their personification an office address on Pete Rose Way.

Watching the playoffs in the early fall of 1986 prompts Bob Howsam to list the big-league managers who, at one time or another, had come under his direction. He gets easily to eleven. "You know Pete Rose will make a fine manager. As a player he always gave 100 percent—more if such a thing is possible. He knows the game, and whatever he does he works at it."

SPARKY: "Pete Rose is an excellent manager. He really knows the game, and he has the temperament for it. I predict he will have the longest tenure of any Cincinnati manager and, before he is through, he will win more games than anyone. These are both records I now hold. He will break them.

"Right now Pete will be setting goals for himself and the team. That's the way he works. He is always setting goals, goals that seem beyond reach. And then he drives himself toward them, reaches them, and then he's always a little sad when he achieves them."

KLU: "Pete stores whole games in his memory. It is unbelievable. I can show him one pitch in a film I've made of him batting in a game, and he can run his own memory backwards or forwards until he tells you the whole game, pitch by pitch.

"Yes, I guess you'd call him a workaholic. He hated—is that too strong?—well anyway, he couldn't stand the days off. He'd come down to the ballpark and take batting practice."

BENCH: "Pete is what he is because of his father, just like I am what I am because of my father."

KENNEDY: "You know, I would fight Pete Rose; I wouldn't ever want to, but if I had to, back to the wall, I would. But I would *never* have fought with Pete's dad. No one would. There was an intensity about that man that was absolutely frightening. . . . "

SPARKY: "I used to call Rose the Animal because of the kind of feverish way he worked out. He'd come out in all kinds of layers of clothing and work up his sweat, and then begin peeling off the clothes, one layer at a time . . . "

EPR: "Rose as an athlete is unique."

HINSCH: "Of all the professional athletes I know about, in all sports, there is only one I'd pay to watch. Pete Rose."

George Anderson and Pete Rose have a lot of mutual respect. Pete says he'd "go through hell in a gasoline suit" for Anderson. One reason the Reds of the 1970s had so much cohesion is that Rose offered Sparky his services as a team leader. Anderson promptly accepted and made Pete the team captain. Perez was the "top dog" when it came to effective ribbing, but Pete—when needed—was something more: a raucous voice in his own style, but a voice from the manager's office. Off the field Rose has, in Sparky's estimation, an unerring instinct for handling people and situations. "There is a time to stand in the corner, keep your mouth shut, and let others have the spotlight. Then there is a time to speak right up and even aggravate people in public. Like the time he told the Los Angeles press the Dodgers were 2 1/2 games ahead chasin' us! But he *always*, and I mean always, knew what was appropriate."

Those who follow sports on television will remember a clubhouse scene following a Rose landmark where considerable difficulty preceded the connection of a phone line from the White House. "This is the President of the United States," Pete was at last informed: "How ya doin'?" opened Rose, putting the man seated next to the Rose Garden at his ease. "I'm sorry I couldn't be there, . . . " began the former sportscaster. "Well, you missed a helluva game . . . "

KENNEDY: "Of all the sports figures I have seen in public life, Rose is the one who never makes a wrong move, who always senses the way to handle a situation."

Pete Rose, being interviewed as a man who now manages, is quick to deflect the personal to the general.

Q: "You have a reputation for expecting players to work hard."

PETE: "I am fortunate to have a bunch of players who take it upon themselves to work their asses off for me. I've got a fine bunch of young players, and they are ready to work their tails off."

Rose proudly and readily accepts his image as Charlie Hustle but adds, "You know people don't realize that all my big ups and downs in this game have come with playoffs and World Series, not from anything I've done myself. There is no way I can describe to you the feeling of being part of a team that wins the World Championship. And there is really nothing like having this feeling for the first time. That's why 1975 will always be the top year for me. We were part of the most exciting World Series ever played, and it was my first experience at being World Champs." Rose was voted MVP for that World Series.

PETE: "Is Cincinnati conservative? If you mean it's not modern, up-to-date, then no. It is just as up-to-date as Philadelphia or Chicago or the other big cities. Cincinnati has some of the best restaurants in the country; it has one of the best zoos—next to San Diego. I always say that Cincinnati has everything the big cities have except for one thing: traffic jams.

Now retired as a player, graying manager Pete Rose still thinks of his home town as "the baseball capital of the world." (Courtesy Cincinnati Reds)

"Of course there are a lot of Germans here, and they are sort of conservative: beer-drinking, hard-working. This is a place where you have to work to get ahead; but if you do there's no problem.

"Does it matter what color you are? Not to me it doesn't; and I've never seen that this was the case around here. There are a lot of people who don't understand Cincinnati, and there's a lot of people who don't *want* to understand this place.

"There are two things wrong with Cincinnati: we don't have a basketball or a hockey team. But I say that because I am such a sports fan. I liked to come down here and see Oscar Robertson and Jack Twyman and those guys; I'd still like to be able to see Julius Erving, Larry Bird, and Magic Johnson.

"We support the Reds tremendously, and we support the Bengals tremendously. Maybe we could give even more support to the teams at Xavier and Cincinnati. But we have this beautiful facility across the street, and we should use it. We should have hockey and the other sports. I was part-owner of the indoor soccer franchise here, and I think we ought to get all the sports we can into these facilities. I mean Cincinnati is such a big-league city, it ought to be big-league in all sports.

"But when I think of this city I think mainly in terms of baseball, 'cause I've been playin' baseball here for so long. I always try to sell Cincinnati as the world capital of baseball. I mean whether I'm playin' in the summer, or goin' on speaking tours in the winter, or traveling to Japan or wherever, I mean this is where the professional game began. We had the first night game. There is more baseball tradition here than anywhere in the world, and that's what I try to point out."

When Pete Rose became eligible for the free-agent draft in 1978, thirteen teams claimed rights to negotiate with him. To prevent his exodus, the city council considered a resolution to make Pete a "historic . . . listed property." Bob Trumpy, former Bengal and popular sports commentator, said this was perfectly proper. If Sadaharu Oh could be declared a national treasure in Japan, then Rose should have equivalent status (*Cincinnati Post*, October 28, 1978, p. 9).

When salary differences with the Reds seemed insoluble, Rose's adviser, Reuven Katz, had no hesitation in taking the case to the public. He knew the citizenry of Cincinnati—even though very few of them made anywhere near what Rose was asking—would back him to the hilt, which they did. Some were not content merely to write management. The media reported a "Keep Pete in Cincy" fund made up of private donations. A high-volume jeweler with stores in Cincinnati and Kentucky opened a

"Let's Get Pete Rose Signed" fund with 10 percent of the gross proceeds of a special discount sale, the funds earmarked for a public charity should Rose refuse them.

BENCH: "This is a city where if they love you they'll forgive you all kinds of things. We have a public figure here who actually paid a lady of the evening with a personal check. He became mayor, and now he's a news anchorman. And so with Pete there have been mega different things—I mean between divorce and paternity suits and all that—and still he is the guy they name streets after."

When, in December of 1978, Rose signed with the Phillies, the newspaper carried a sympathetic interview giving his particular reasons for choosing Philadelphia over others that had offered more money. That same issue (*Cincinnati Post*, December 5, 1978) carried Pete's record at the top of the sports section and featured a full page of citizen quotations under the heading "Good Luck, Pete." The general tone of these remarks was that, although Rose was "foolish to give up his roots," the team should have paid him more.

When Rose finally left, it fell to Ray Knight, a scrappy and timely-hitting product of the Reds' farm system, to replace him at third. Even Pete's booster, Sparky, calls Rose "a jackhammer third baseman: he was crude, but he worked at it." "Third base was my position," points out Knight. "I'd been playing there all my life. Pete came there only after spending most of his career at other positions. But that didn't matter to the fans. Every time a ball would get by me, 'Pete woulda got it,' they'd holler. It took two years, including a year of hitting over .300, for me to win them over. And even then I was never sure.

"It is tough to try replacing a legend. Cincinnati people are not very tolerant of nonconformity, but they were flexible enough to forgive Pete his peccadillos."

There are those who seem bewildered at the gradual and unspectacular ways Rose-the-manager has allowed Rose-the-player to fade from the scene. In 1987 there was talk Pete might activate himself for the League Championship Series; but the Reds didn't make it. As they played out their card, heading for another second-place finish, the Reds' owner—clearly interested in ticket sales—petitioned Pete to give the younger fans a chance to see him in action. He politely declined.

Although it has attracted little notice, Pete Rose's last appearance marked a very special occasion. It was a day, August 17, 1986, when the manager was starting an intermittently sore-armed pitcher, Chris Welsh, who also happened to be an alumnus of the local St. Xavier High School.

At shortstop and third crouched Larkin and Bell, both of whom once attended Moeller High and, on the other side of second, was Ron Oester, pride of Withrow. In right field, as usual, loomed the former Courter Tech slugger, Dave Parker. What was apparently the final appearance of Pete Rose's magnificent career came as a pinch-hitter in this game, bringing to six the number of native sons playing for the Reds that day: that day and *only* that day.

Q: "What do you think of this highly unusual situation where you have six hometown players on the same team?"

PETE: "I think it's great for the city."

KATZ: "Wherever you were with Pete, 'we' and 'us' always meant the Reds. Even when he was playing for Philadelphia or Montreal, Cincinnati was always home."

KENNEDY: "I guess you could call Pete Rose the quintessential Cincinnati Dutchman."

KEY TO INTERVIEWS

Individuals quoted frequently have been designated in abbreviated fashion as follows:

BELL: David Gus "Buddy" Bell grew up in Cincinnati (Moeller High), son of Reds centerfielder Gus Bell. Buddy played third base for Cleveland and Texas for thirteen years before coming to the Reds in July, 1985.

BENCH: Johnny Bench played for the Reds 1967–83; has remained a Cincinnati resident, active in the media.

CONCEPCION: David Concepcion has played for the Reds since 1970.

EPR: Eugene Ruehlmann, prominent Cincinnati attorney, served on the city council, including two terms as mayor. He was a decisive force in building and locating Riverfront Stadium.

HINSCH: Warren K. Hinsch, widely known local insurance agent with strong interests in sports and local politics.

HOWSAM: Robert L. Howsam, nationally known sports executive, acquired by the Reds in 1967 to design their entire operation.

KATZ: Reuven Katz is a trust attorney with a long-standing interest in representing athletes. His clients include Bench, Perez, and Rose.

KENNEDY: Edward J. Kennedy, native Cincinnatian, former assistant to announcer Waite Hoyt, and well-known sportscaster throughout the area.

KLU: Ted Kluzewski, an all-time local favorite, played first base for the Reds 1947–57, then elsewhere. Returned to Reds as hitting coach until his retirement announced in January, '88.

KNIGHT: Ray Knight, third baseman for several teams, came up through the Reds farm system and had the unenviable task of replacing Rose when Pete left for Philadelphia.

LARKIN: Barry Larkin, native son (Moeller High), product of Reds farms system who became starting shortstop in 1987.

OESTER: Ron Oester, born in Cincinnati (Withrow High), emerged from Reds farm clubs in 1980 to become regular second baseman until serious knee injury in 1987.

PARKER: Dave Parker, raised in Cincinnati (Courter Tech), played many games against the Reds (for Pittsburgh) before joining them, 1984–87.

PEREZ: Atanasio "Tony" Perez, known as Big Doggie for his leadership in the clubhouse and with the bat, played for the Reds 1964–76, returned in '84, retired to a coaching position at the end of the '86 season.

PETE: Peter Edward "Charlie Hustle" Rose, as *The Baseball Encyclopedia* lists him, *The Sporting News* Athlete of the Decade in the '70s, and the city's sporting emblem. Rose grew up in Cincinnati (Western Hills High), played for the Reds 1963–77, and returned as playing manager in 1984.

ROBINSON: Brooks Robinson, Hall of Fame Baltimore third baseman, teamed with former Red Frank Robinson to defeat the Reds in the '70 Series. Presently commentator on Oriole telecasts.

SPARKY: George "Sparky" Anderson managed the Big Red Machine 1970–77; now manages the Detroit Tigers.

STOWE: Bernie Stowe grew up in Cincinnati's West End, started as visiting team batboy while still in school. Now equipment manager; has been with the team for forty years.

WELSH: Chris Welsh, native son (Xavier High), pitched for several major-league teams, including the Reds in 1986.

All of the above-named individuals were subjects of tape-recorded interviews made in Cincinnati mostly during the summer of 1986. A few interviews occurred elsewhere during the summer and fall of 1986 and at Tampa during spring training, 1987. Others were interviewed, sometimes more than once. What they said comes from notes and memory. Although they are not frequently quoted, they provided much useful background. They are:

Ethan ALLEN, Cincinnati native who played for East High and the University of Cincinnati, then began with the Reds in 1926 a major-league career that lasted twenty-two years with a lifetime batting average of exactly .300. Coach at Yale for twenty years, Allen is now retired in Chapel Hill, N.C.

Thomas BOSWELL, sports journalist who wrote about the Reds of the 1970s and has published two collections of baseball essays.

Gordy COLEMAN played first base for the 1960–67 Reds and now heads their Speakers Bureau.

David S. ECKER, outstanding athlete in school and college, lifelong Cincinnati resident, manufacturing and sales consultant.

Jim FERGUSON, former sportswriter in charge of Reds publicity since 1972.

Mrs. Waite HOYT, widow of the great pitcher and popular broadcaster; secretary to Warren Giles when he was president of the National league.

John F. KOONS, lifelong Cincinnatian, manages soft-drink and investment companies. He succeeded his father as president of Burger Beer and Midland Advertising just as baseball/beer merchandising was entering a new era.

John MURDOUGH, former business manager of both the Bengals and the Reds.

Mr. and Mrs. Louis and Louise NIPPERT are among a small group of the most influential and civic-minded Cincinnatians. Among their shared interests are music and sports. Lou Nippert brought Bob Howsam to Cincinnati; both Nipperts are minority owners of the present Reds.

Glenn REDMER, Supervisor of Riverfront Stadium.

Joseph ROCHFORD, Director of Cincinnati Public Utilities.

NOTE ON SOURCES

Although the interest in this work rests mainly on what those interviewed had to say, it was necessary to supplement this information with related materials. The list that follows is not exhaustive, nor does it necessarily represent the best sources. It is a record of what I found—with considerable help—to be useful in understanding the subject and includes all works quoted or cited.

For general information, and sometimes for pictures, I used the files of the daily press, the *Enquirer*, and the *Post-Times Star, The Sporting News*, press releases and house publications such as *Redsvue* and *Reds Report*; also the files of the Cincinnati Historical Society, the Cincinnati Public Library, the Cincinnati Reds, the Greater Cincinnati Convention and Visitors Bureau, the photograph collection of Strauss & Troy, and the archives of the University of Cincinnati.

Among the many important books on Cincinnati, my subject indebted me to the Cincinnati City Planning Commission's *The Cincinnati Metropolitan Master Plan and the Official Plan* adopted November 22, 1948, the one-volume version; Carl W. Condit, *The Railroad and the City* (Columbus: Ohio State University Press, 1977); Laurence C. Gerckens, "Bettman of Cincinnati," in Donald A Krueckeberg, ed., *The American Planner* (New York: Methuen, 1983); Daniel Hurley, *Cincinnati: The Queen City* (Cincinnati: The Cincinnati Historical Society, 1982); Walter C. Langsam, *Cincinnati in Color* (New York: Hastings House, 1978). Of the several interpretive works of Zane L. Miller, I am most indebted to *Boss Cox's Cincinnati* (New York: Oxford, 1968) and "History and the Politics of Community Change in Cincinnati," *Public Historian* 5 (Fall, '83): 17–35.

Also on the city: Steven J. Ross, *Workers on the Edge* (New York: Columbia University Press, 1985); Mel Scott, *American City Planning since 1980* (Berkeley: University of California Press, 1971); Iola Silberstein, *Cincinnati Then and Now* (Cincinnati: League of Women Voters, 1982); Robert I. Vexler, ed., *Cincinnati: A Chronological and Documentary History* (Dobbs Ferry, N.Y.: Oceana, 1975); and the unpublished essay of Joseph Rochford, "The Games Cities Play: Cincinnati's Decision to Build Riverfront Stadium."

To learn more about beer in the Queen City, I read Susan K. Appel, "Buildings and Beer: Brewery Architecture of Cincinnati," *Queen City Heritage* 44 (Summer, 1986): 3–20; William L. Downard, *The Cincinnati Brewing Industry* (Athens: Ohio University Press, 1973); and the undated pamphlet produced by the Hudepohl Brewing Company, "Brewing in Cincinnati, 1885–1985."

Concerning the local German heritage, there were Kathy Doane, "Does Our German Image Still Fit?" *Tristate Magazine*, September 8, 1985, pp. 4 and continuations; G. A. Dobbert, "The Cincinnati Germans, 1870–1920," *Bulletin of the Cincinnati Historical Society* 23 (October, 1965): 229–42; the Fall, 1984, number of *Queen City Heritage*, which is entirely devoted to the German ethnicity of the region; and two of Don Heinrich Tolzmann's works: *The Cincinnati Germans after the Great War* (New York: Lang, 1987) and *The Festschrift for the German-American Tricentennial Jubilee, Cincinnati, 1983*, which he edited for the Cincinnati Historical Society (no date).

The only treatment of a sport other than baseball that sharpened my focus was Clifford Geertz, "Deep Play: Notes on the Balinese Cockfight," *Daedalus* 101 (Winter, 1972): 1–37. While they contain little about the Reds, Thomas Boswell's *How Life Imitates the World Series* (New York: Doubleday, 1982) and *Why Time Begins Opening Day* (New York: Doubleday, 1984) furnished original perspectives. Some parts of Peter Golenbock's *Bums: An Oral History of the Brooklyn Dodgers* (New York: Putnam, 1984) came close to the treatment of the baseball context I was attempting. In a very different way, so did Stephen Hardy, *How Boston Played* (Boston: Northeastern University Press, 1982). The best model for identifying baseball with a specific culture I found to be Robert Whiting, *The Chrysanthemum and the Bat: The Game the Japanese Play* (Tokyo: Permanent Press, 1977). Daniel Okrent, in *Nine Innings* (New York: Ticknor & Fields, 1985), provides a nice model for relating the play of the game to the background and forethought.

These books were useful to me for their discussion of baseball's economics and for relating finances to motivation and fan response: Bowie Kuhn, with Martin Appel, *Hardball* (New York: Times Books, 1987); Leo Lowenfish and Tony Lupien, *The Imperfect Diamond* (New York: Stein & Day, 1980); and David Q. Voigt, *American Baseball*, vol. 3 (University Park: Penn State University Press, 1983).

Two books cover the Reds' history over long periods of time and do so very well: for the earliest days, Harry Ellard, *Baseball in Cincinnati: A History* (Cincinnati: privately printed, 1907). Lee Allen takes up where Ellard left off and carries the story through the early 1940s in *The Cincinnati Reds* (New York: Putnam, 1948). Other germane historical treatments included articles and papers by Kevin Grace such as " 'Bushel Basket' Charlie Gould of the Red Stockings" in the 1984 *SABR Baseball Research Journal*, pp. 82–84; Jack Selzer, *Baseball in the Nineteenth Century: An Overview* (Cooperstown: SABR, 1986); Philip J. Lowry, *Green Cathedrals* (Cooperstown: SABR, 1986); Donal Spivey, ed., *Sport in America: New Historical Perspectives* (Westport, Conn.: Greenwood, 1985), especially Carl M. Becker and Richard H. Grigsby, "Baseball in the Small Ohio Community, 1865–1900," pp. 77–93; and David Q. Voigt, "America's First Red Scare—The Cincinnati Reds of 1869," *Ohio History* 78 (Winter, 1969): 13–24.

On the Reds of the 1970s, I made use of Sparky Anderson and Si Burick, *The Main Spark* (New York: Doubleday, 1978); Ritter Collett, *Men of the Reds Machine* (Dayton, Ohio: Landfall Press, 1977); John Erardi, *Pete Rose 4192* (Cincinnati: Enquirer, 1985); Bob Hertzel, *The Big Red Machine* (Englewood Cliffs, N.J.: Prentice Hall, 1976); Hal McCoy, *The Relentless Reds* (Shelbyville, Ky.: PressCo, 1976); Joe Morgan, with Joel H. Cohen, *Baseball My Way* (New York: Atheneum, 1976); Bob Rathgeber, *Cincinnati Reds Scrapbook* (Virginia Beach, Va.: JCP, 1982); Pete Rose, with Bob Hertzel, *Charlie Hustle* (Englewood Cliffs, N.J.: Prentice Hall, 1975); and Pete Rose, *The Pete Rose Story* (New York: World, 1970).

INDEX

ROBERT HARRIS "HUB" WALKER, a Cincinnati native, has been a member of the George Washington University faculty for thirty years. He served as president of the American Studies Association and edited its two leading journals. Among his published works are American Society, Reform in America, and Everyday Life in the Age of Enterprise.